Connecting Central Asia with Economic Centers

A Study of the Asian Development Bank Institute

Printed using vegetable oil-based inks on recycled paper; manufactured through a
totally chlorine-free process.

ISBN 978-4-89974-049-0 (Print)
ISBN 978-4-89974-050-6 (PDF)

Cover photograph by Shoko Muraguchi

Asian Development Bank Institute
Kasumigaseki Building 8F
3-2-5, Kasumigaseki, Chiyoda-ku
Tokyo 100-6008, Japan
www.adbi.org

Contents

Contents

Boxes, Figures, and Tables

Tables

Foreword

There is increasing policy and academic interest in the economic connections between Central Asia and major economic centers. These have increased over the years, driven by economic growth, falling trade barriers, improvements to infrastructure and logistics, and production networks. The progress of integration between Central Asia and major economic centers seems likely to accelerate in coming years and has the potential to contribute to inclusive and equitable growth in Asia and the Pacific.

The Asian Development Bank Institute (ADBI) has been supporting regional cooperation and integration for economic and social development in Asia. The current study is part of this effort and aims to broaden understanding of the links between Central Asia and the People's Republic of China, Japan, the Republic of Korea, the Russian Federation, and the United States, and with associations of countries such as the Association of Southeast Asian Nations (ASEAN) and the European Union. ADBI researchers and regional experts worked together on this project. This report describes the pattern of economic integration between Central Asia and major economic centers, analyzes the factors driving the growing trade and financial ties, examines the benefits and costs of integration, and provides policy recommendations for improving Central Asia's participation in regional cooperation and integration.

The study finds that there has been strong growth in trade and investment ties between the economies of Central Asia and major economic centers over the past two decades. Extraction industries and related services are key to the existing economic integration in the resource-rich economies (Kazakhstan, Turkmenistan, and Uzbekistan), while worker remittances continue to provide a major source of revenues for the non-resource-rich economies (Kyrgyz Republic and Tajikistan). While there are advantages for Central Asia in focusing on core sectors where countries enjoy a comparative advantage, there is also scope to strengthen the positive spillovers to other parts of the economy. Governments need to provide the appropriate support for adjustment across sectors that will come as a result of economic openness, lower trade barriers, and free trade agreements. The study finds that economic diversification, exploration into new industries, and participation in global production networks are being developed concurrently as a strategic part of economic integration with major economic centers.

Eight policy recommendations emerge from this study:

(i) Behind-the-border reforms are needed.
(ii) Sound management of macroeconomic policies is essential.
(iii) Sustainable trade openness will facilitate the evolution of comparative advantages and diversification of markets over time.
(iv) Regional trade integration can complement World Trade Organization (WTO) membership and multilateral trade rules.
(v) Inward foreign direct investment (FDI) has facilitated the exploration of Central Asia's energy and natural resources, but positive spillovers to other sectors are yet to occur.
(vi) Investments in cross-border land infrastructure to improve quality and streamline trade facilitation will reduce trade costs in landlocked Central Asian economies and facilitate trade growth.
(vii) Market-oriented economic policies need to be coherent and predictable to support economic and market diversification.
(viii) Financial inclusion and social safety nets need to be strengthened.

We hope that this study will deepen our knowledge of the increasing regional and global economic connectivity of Central Asia.

Naoyuki Yoshino

Naoyuki Yoshino
Dean and CEO
Asian Development Bank Institute

Acknowledgments

This final report was prepared under the overall guidance of Jae-Ha Park (Deputy Dean, ADBI) and Ganeshan Wignaraja (Director of Research, ADBI). Yothin Jinjarak (Research Fellow, ADBI) was the task manager for the report, Roman Mogilevskii (Senior Research Fellow, University of Central Asia) was the lead consultant, and Richard Pomfret (Professor, University of Adelaide) was a consultant.

The report was written by a team of ADBI staff and consultants. The chapters were prepared based on inputs from Roman Mogilevskii, Richard Pomfret, Yothin Jinjarak, and Ganeshan Wignaraja. Paulo Jose Mutuc, Ny You, and Umid Abidhadjaev provided research assistance while Yoshi Nakayama, Yasuyo Sugihara, and Mikiko Tanaka provided administrative support. Robert Davis (Communications Specialist, ADBI) and his team prepared the report for publication. Grant Stillman (Legal Adviser, ADBI) dealt with contractual matters.

The report has also benefited from support and technical comments from staff from the Asian Development Bank (ADB) and ADBI as well as external experts. These include the following from ADB and ADBI: Klaus Gerhaeusser (Director General, Central and West Asia Department, ADB), Vicky C.L. Tan (Director, Regional Cooperation and Operations Coordination Division, Central and West Asia Department, ADB), and Pradeep Srivastava (Principal Economist, Regional Cooperation and Operations Coordination Division, Central and West Asia Department, ADB), Masahiro Kawai (former Dean of ADBI), Giovanni Capannelli (Special Adviser to the Dean, ADBI), Peter Morgan (Senior Consultant for Research, ADBI), Matthias Helble (Research Fellow, ADBI), Victor Pontines (Research Fellow, ADBI), Menaka Arudchelvan (Project Consultant, ADBI), Jenny Balboa (Project Consultant, ADBI), and Xiaoming Pan (Project Consultant, ADBI).

Johannes Linn (Senior Resident Scholar, Emerging Markets Forum; Non-Resident Senior Fellow, Brookings Institution) provided peer review comments on the report.

Valuable technical comments were also provided by experts at the workshops in Tokyo, Astana, and Tashkent. We are particularly grateful to the following experts: Timur Dadabaev (Associate Professor, Graduate School of Social Sciences and Humanities, Special Program for Central Asian Countries, University of Tsukuba, Japan), Mila Kashcheeva (Researcher, Inter-disciplinary Studies Center, Technological Innovation and Economic Growth Studies Group, Institute of Developing Economies, Japan External Trade Organization, Japan), Atsushi Masuda (Japan Bank for International Cooperation, Japan), Tetsuji Tanaka (Vice President/Executive Director, Central Asia and Caucasus Research Institute, Japan), and Tetsuya Yamada (Director, Central Asia and the Caucasus Division, East and Central Asia and the Caucasus Department, Japan International Cooperation Agency, Japan).

The following experts contributed inputs to the text boxes and provided comments on the report: Shokhboz Asadov (Institute of Public Policy and Administration, University of Central Asia, Tajikistan), Ildus Kamilov (Center for Economic Research, Uzbekistan), Maruert Makhmutova (Public Policy Research, Kazakhstan), and Kubat Umurzakov (Investment Roundtable, Kyrgyz Republic).

For further information about the study, the following may be contacted:

Ganeshan Wignaraja (Director of Research, ADBI)
E-mail: gwignaraja@adbi.org

Yothin Jinjarak (Research Fellow, ADBI)
E-mail: yjinjarak@adbi.org

About This Study

This is the final report of the Asian Development Bank Institute (ADBI) study "Connecting Central Asia with Economic Centers." The study focuses on the five Central Asian economies: Kazakhstan, the Kyrgyz Republic, Tajikistan, Turkmenistan, and Uzbekistan. The aim of the report is to (i) examine the pattern of economic relationships between these economies and major economic centers since their transition to the market economy in the early 1990s, (ii) highlight emerging challenges, and (iii) explore policy implications. It covers trade ties, foreign direct investment and financial flows, migration and remittances, and institutional cooperation between Central Asian economies and major economic centers, including those in Asia, the European Union, the Russian Federation, and the United States.

This is the first empirical study of Central Asia by ADBI. Based largely on desk research and analysis of data, interactions with regional experts, and a technical workshop in Tokyo (10 March 2014), a technical workshop in Astana (5 May 2014), and a presentation in Tashkent (6 June 2014), it is intended as a stocktaking exercise for future ADBI research on the economic development of Central Asia. The report includes text boxes on the progress of transition, tariff protection in Central Asia, tourism in Central Asia, garment exports in the Kyrgyz Republic, the financial sector in Kazakhstan, the role of Uzbekistan in regional transport and as a transit hub, labor migration from Tajikistan, and the development priorities of oil and non-oil exporters.

The report is structured as follows. Chapter 1 provides a macroeconomic overview of Central Asia from 1990 to the present, covering the two decades of transition. Chapter 2 examines trade ties between Central Asia and economic centers. Chapter 3 analyzes foreign direct investment links. Chapter 4 examines finance, infrastructure, migration, institutions, and other links. Chapter 5 explores key policy implications from the research.

Overview

This study aims to provide a systematic analysis of the economic relationships—trade ties, foreign direct investment links, financial flows, and institutional cooperation—between the Central Asian republics and global economic centers in Asia, the European Union, the Russian Federation, and the United States. Trade and investment flows between the Central Asian region and the economic centers have increased markedly over recent years, driven by resource complementarities, demand conditions, and regional cooperation initiatives. The forces of globalization and the recovery of the world economy from the crisis of 2008–2009 imply that economic ties between Central Asia and the rest of the world are likely to strengthen.

The potential rapid expansion of economic ties between Central Asia and economic centers will produce opportunities and policy challenges. During the transition to greater economic ties, adjustment issues may arise from resource transfers between sectors and countries, employment reallocations, and production relocations that will affect particular countries and industries. Gaps in transportation infrastructure, trade facilitation, energy security, migration, and financial sector development, among others, may impede the expansion of such economic ties. There are also underexplored issues of trade and foreign direct investment between Central Asia and the economic centers, including production networks, technology transfers, impediments to further market integration, and the future of economic cooperation, all of which can affect the prospects for inclusive and sustainable growth in Central Asia.

Growth, Openness, and Structural Change

After gaining independence in 1991, the new countries of Central Asia went through painful transitions to market economies and experienced significant economic decline and increased poverty. The transition required a dramatic change in the industrial structure of these economies, including a sharp contraction of manufacturing in all of them. In the process of transition, all the countries managed to maintain quite developed social systems, providing universal access to secondary education, health care, and pension insurance. By 2000, this adjustment had been mostly completed, and the countries started to grow. In 2000–2012, Central Asia grew much faster than the global economy, allowing incomes to increase and poverty to be substantially reduced. However, the performance of the countries was quite diverse in terms of their economic development levels and models, despite their similar histories and cultures.

An important driver of Central Asia's economic growth in the 21st century has been a very significant increase in international prices for energy and metals, resources which are abundant in Central Asia. High resource prices attracted massive foreign direct investment (FDI) into oil and gas extraction industries and transport infrastructure, which led to rapid export growth in hydrocarbon-rich countries (Kazakhstan, Turkmenistan, and Uzbekistan). Even the countries that lack substantial hydrocarbon deposits (Kyrgyz Republic and Tajikistan) benefited from this price increase through the remittances of their migrants to oil-rich neighboring countries (Russian Federation and Kazakhstan).

Two decades of intensive economic change—first negative, then positive—led to major structural changes in these economies. Mining and non-tradable services are now key drivers of economic growth and the largest sectors in all five countries. Agriculture, which used to be a key economic sector and main employer in Central Asia, is no longer as important as it was, although it remains a significant source of living for the predominantly rural populations of Central Asia. However, agriculture can regain its role as an economic driver if reforms are implemented and connections to regional and global markets are improved. The growth of manufacturing varies from country to country, but in all economies of the region manufacturing plays a secondary role to oil and gas, mining, and non-tradable services.

The emphasis on exports of natural resources has helped to open these economies and many channels now link them to the global economy, including trade in goods and services, FDI, labor migration and migrants' remittances, and official development assistance. Data show a strong positive correlation between the economic performance of Central Asian countries and the intensity of their external links.

However, their specialization on exports of natural resources and labor has increased these economies' dependence on a few global markets and inhibited the development of manufacturing and other potentially tradable sectors in Central Asia. Economic diversification is now a central item on the policy agenda in all Central Asia.

While the per capita incomes have increased and the proportion of the population in poverty has declined over most of the last two decades, more research is needed into poverty reduction, income inequality, and social safety nets and their implications for economic empowerment.

Trade Expansion and Concentration

Since 2000, Kazakhstan, Turkmenistan, and Uzbekistan have demonstrated impressive export and import growth in both monetary and physical terms. However, in all five countries, exports have become concentrated on very few primary commodities (crude oil, natural gas, oil products, ferrous and non-ferrous metals, cotton, and wheat). Exports of more sophisticated manufactured products and services are not large, with the exception of exports of automobiles from Uzbekistan and tourism services from the Kyrgyz Republic. Central Asia's imports consist mostly of manufactured products, energy, transportation, and engineering and construction services.

Geographically, exports are also concentrated on a small number of markets: the People's Republic of China (PRC), the European Union, and the Russian Federation. In particular, the PRC is a major economic partner of Central Asia for both exports and imports. The five countries are also gradually reorienting their exports and imports toward Turkey, Iran, the Republic of Korea, and other Asian partners.

To what extent is diversification of trade necessary for Central Asia? On the one hand, greater product differentiation, both horizontally (number of products) and vertically (quality of products), would increase trade ties with major economic centers at the higher end of economic development and expand Central Asia's market destinations. On the other, Central Asia also needs to increase production and exports in its area of comparative advantage, taking into account the fixed costs and increasing returns available in such core sectors as oil, gas, and mineral extraction, as well as manufacturing sectors that require high capital intensity and entry barriers. More data on consumption patterns and home-market effects on exports and imports, and the conflicting forces of factor proportions and product differentiation of the comparative advantage of Central Asia, are needed to determine the optimum extent of diversification.

Inflow of Foreign Direct Investment

The countries of Central Asia differ significantly in their approaches to FDI. Energy-rich countries with favorable regimes for foreign investments (Kazakhstan and Turkmenistan) managed to attract substantial amounts of FDI and have entered the ranks of the top investment destinations in Asia and in the world.

The two main motives for FDI to come to Central Asia are to seek natural resources (e.g., energy and metals) and new markets in non-tradable sectors (e.g., real estate development and retail). Many Central Asian countries have substantial national savings, so their motive in attracting FDI is primarily to benefit from investors' technologies and expertise. However, technology transfer has been very limited so far.

Agriculture and labor-intensive manufacturing receive little investment. Central Asia's participation in global value chains is mostly limited to supplies of natural resources and labor; there are few examples of more complex intermediate or final tasks being undertaken in the region.

FDI has enabled the expansion of extraction industries and non-tradable services, and export growth, all of which are a major source of government revenue. The employment impacts of FDI are much less significant.

Financial, Institutional, and Other External Links

There are a number of other links between Central Asia and the global economies. These include financial flows, official development assistance, transport and transit, migration and remittances, and institutional links.

Apart from flows associated with trade and FDI, another major financial stream is portfolio investments by Kazakhstan's National Fund and by a similar institution in Turkmenistan. Apart from those in Kazakhstan, the financial sectors of Central Asia are not significantly integrated into global financial markets. The financial markets are generally underdeveloped and there is heavy state involvement in most Central Asian countries.

The financial crisis of 2008–2009 exposed the vulnerability of the financial sector in several countries in Central Asia. The banking crisis of Kazakhstan in 2009 complicated the government's budgetary position and diverted resources that could otherwise have been used to promote economic growth. In future, Central Asia will have to take into account the interdependence of the financial sector, monetary policy, and exchange rate stabilization, together with the level of dollarization, growth in consumer borrowing, and inadequacy of lending to small and medium-sized enterprises. Central Asian countries are small open economies and need to put in place macro-prudential policies that take into account externalities from foreign economic shocks as well as potential currency depreciation, and possible competitive devaluation, from major trading partners and other economies supplying similar exporting commodities, all of which could have significant effects on the cross-border flows of trade and foreign investment.

Official development assistance, which was an important source of foreign exchange for these countries in the 1990s, was less important in the 2000s, although it remains significant for costly and technically complex infrastructure projects.

Central Asian countries have made a major effort to diversify their transport routes and energy links (especially through pipelines) and to connect their economies not only with the Russian Federation to the north, but also with the PRC and other southern neighbors. Automobile and railway transport infrastructure development is coordinated regionally under the auspices of the Central Asia Regional Economic Cooperation (CAREC) program. Kazakhstan and some other countries of the region have made major investments in order to become part of a Eurasian land bridge joining the dynamic markets surrounding Central Asia.

The oil boom of the 2000s contributed to the growth of wages in the Russian Federation and Kazakhstan and created some room in these two countries' labor markets for migrants from the Kyrgyz Republic, Tajikistan, and Uzbekistan. This significantly eased the labor market situation in the countries sending migrants and provided major support to household livelihoods in these countries through remittances. In Tajikistan and the Kyrgyz Republic, remittances are more important than export revenue; these two countries occupy two first places in the world based on their remittances to gross domestic product ratio. While undoubtedly positive in the short and medium term, labor out-migration in the long term is associated with leakage of skilled workers from these economies, and imposes social risks and costs including migrants' often poor living conditions, labor safety, and the impact on child care in their families.

Regional cooperation and the countries' integration into the global trade system are important issues. Regional disintegration (rather than integration) has been the trend in Central Asia until recently. The customs union of Belarus, Kazakhstan, and the Russian Federation is a new initiative with the potential to create and divert trade and other external economic flows in the region depending on the degree of progress in trade facilitation between the Russian Federation and Kazakhstan and between Kazakhstan and its southern neighbors. There are plans to convert the customs union into a Eurasian Union by 2015; the Kyrgyz Republic and Tajikistan are considering joining this customs union. At the same time, the Russian Federation and Tajikistan recently joined the World Trade Organization (WTO), and Kazakhstan plans to join soon. The expansion prospect of the customs union implies that further consideration of the trade creation and trade diversion, as well as the analysis of the effects of the customs union on the export and import patterns, factors of production, and employment is crucial for the members, potential members, and non-members alike.

Policy Implications

If countries are to diversify their economies, they need to produce products that are competitive in domestic, regional, and global markets.

"Behind-the-border" reforms are needed. These include improvements to governance and the business climate, investments in hard and soft infrastructure, financial support for small and medium-sized enterprises, and better education and health services.

Sound management of macroeconomic policies is essential. Lower inflation would help countries to become more competitive. This implies careful use of monetary policy, but, more importantly, structural reforms to increase competition and reduce transaction costs. Prudent fiscal policy, expanding the tax base, and ensuring exchange rates are consistent with economic fundamentals are all important to strengthen the resilience of Central Asian economies against exogenous shocks.

Sustainable trade openness will facilitate the evolution of comparative advantages and diversification of markets over time. Lowering tariffs and taking non-tariff measures will help countries to integrate themselves into the global trade system, which is essential for countries aspiring to become producers and exporters of more diversified products. WTO membership supports openness at the national level by providing a rules-based multilateral trading system which treats large and small countries alike. With Kazakhstan's WTO accession expected in 2014 or 2015, Turkmenistan and Uzbekistan will remain the only countries in the region still far from WTO membership. In these countries, the gradual phaseout of some protection measures and harmonization of remaining ones with the forms and levels usual for WTO members need to be planned and implemented systematically. Entry into free trade agreements and multilateral negotiations also have important implications for structural adjustment across industries and sectors. The development and resilience of garment exports in the Kyrgyz Republic and the challenges introduced by the expected accession of the Kyrgyz Republic to the customs union of Belarus, Kazakhstan, and the Russian Federation provides a case in point.

Regional trade integration can complement WTO membership and multilateral trade rules. Regional preferential trade agreements (including the customs union of Belarus, Kazakhstan, and the Russian Federation) may contribute to Central Asia's economic diversification but they need to be carefully managed. Their usefulness is positively correlated with their capacity to facilitate trade among the participants and to open the large Russian market for Central Asian producers and negatively correlated with the extent of trade diversion they cause. The future evolution and net economic benefits of the customs union are still uncertain and require further research. It will be important for non-oil exporters like the Kyrgyz Republic and Tajikistan which are considering accession to this union to integrate labor migration issues into their accession plans and to invest in capacity building for negotiating and implementing trade policy.

Not only the amount, but also the quality of FDI has created opportunities in the region. Inward FDI has facilitated the exploration of Central Asia's energy and natural resources, but positive spillovers to other sectors are yet to occur. Development of new, more advanced products requires investment, both domestic and FDI. All governments have friendly FDI-attraction policies, but many of these policies are discretionary, which may mean that they turn away smaller but innovative foreign investors in knowledge- or labor-intensive sectors. The amount of realized FDI is directly correlated with the expected rate of return on investments, which means that (i) investors must be allowed to make profits, and (ii) the probability of project failure must be reduced by providing a regulatory environment free of non-market risks. As technology and expertise transfer is one of the most important benefits brought in by FDI, it is essential that domestic workers have the education and training to benefit from such transfers. At the same time, a transition to manufacturing or service activities providing jobs for better educated segments of the labor force should not exclude those currently employed in informal trade or semi-subsistence agriculture.

Investments in cross-border land infrastructure to improve quality and streamline trade facilitation will reduce trade costs in landlocked Central Asian economies and facilitate trade growth. Further development of the transport infrastructure is an important prerequisite for greater integration of Central Asia into the global economy. However, physical infrastructure alone will be insufficient. Apart from the high level of trade costs, the current state of logistics in the region leads to unpredictable costs and scheduling. Reforms in the management of cross-border and multimodal shipments, technical and administrative compliance with existing standards and norms, and ending artificial barriers aimed at extorting side payments from freight operators are among the prerequisites for developing the region's transit potential and improving the prospects of integrating Central Asia into the global economy beyond the role of primary product exporters. The Central Asian economies should benefit from the development of additional multimodal transport and logistics hubs in the region, as has been proven successfully for the Navoi transport and industrial hub in Uzbekistan.

Coherence and predictability of market-oriented economic policy is essential to support economic and market diversification. Hard and soft infrastructure must improve in tandem, and the latter requires improved governance and ease of doing business. Transport infrastructure projects are very expensive, and investment can be wasted if attention is not paid to their consistency with other external economic policies. Construction of a Eurasian land bridge and of trans-regional pipelines requires regional cooperation or there is a risk that expensive projects will end up as white elephants. If Central Asian countries wish to participate in the global value chains that are the most dynamic segment of the 21st century global economy, they must improve the ease of doing business and the predictability and cost of international transactions, especially in connection with manufacturing centers of Asia.

Financial inclusion and social safety nets need to be strengthened. Economic openness can bring welfare improvements and benefits to Central Asian economies, as well as economic and social (job displacement) costs as they adjust to their integration into global markets. Most producers and firms in the region only supply domestic markets, which means there is much room for increasing trade. However, access to credit for small and medium-sized firms is needed for firms to upgrade their production and to enable them to join production networks and to overcome the sunk cost barriers to enter foreign markets. Broad-based and targeted credit schemes for domestic firms, including low interest rates, attainable collateral requirements, and an efficient loan application process, are needed, particularly for the non-exporting firms in Central Asia. For both oil-exporting countries and non-oil-exporting countries, questions remain to what degree the diversification of trade is necessary for Central Asia. On the one hand, greater product differentiation, both horizontally (number of products) and vertically (quality of products), would help firms in Central Asia to increase their trade ties with major economic centers at higher levels of economic development and to expand market destinations. On the other, Central Asia also needs to increase production and exports in the areas of its comparative advantage, taking into account the fixed costs and increasing returns in such core sectors as oil, gas, and mineral extraction, as well as in manufacturing sectors that require high capital intensity and have entry barriers. The question of diversification is important both for oil-exporting countries because of increasing returns to scale to achieve lower average costs in their core competitive sectors, and for the non-oil-exporting countries, where labor markets are tightly linked with business cycles in foreign countries and incomes from workers' remittances from abroad.

In this regard, the non-oil-exporting countries need to strengthen their social safety nets. As can be seen in Tajikistan, remittances are a key driver of economic development and poverty reduction. The oil-exporting countries also need to improve social security measures, making prudent use of oil and commodity revenues. Increasing the population's access to financial services and improving the competitiveness of the financial sector (as is currently being done in Kazakhstan) should help to enhance financial inclusion in the Central Asian economies.

Abbreviations

ADB	–	Asian Development Bank
ADBI	–	Asian Development Bank Institute
ASEAN	–	Association of Southeast Asian Nations
BRIC	–	Brazil, the Russian Federation, India, and the People's Republic of China
CAREC	–	Central Asia Regional Economic Cooperation
EU	–	European Union
EurAsEc	–	Eurasian Economic Community
FDI	–	foreign direct investment
GDP	–	gross domestic product
PRC	–	People's Republic of China
SPECA	–	Special Programme for the Economies of Central Asia
UN Comtrade	–	United Nations Commodity Trade Statistics Database
US	–	United States
WTO	–	World Trade Organization

1. Macroeconomic Overview of Central Asia

1.1   Introduction

This chapter examines the macroeconomic development of Central Asia. The focus is on the recovery in economic growth and production during the 1990s and the 2000s. Growth patterns, the region's economic performance compared with that of other parts of the world, production structures, macroeconomic indicators, labor market conditions, and patterns of economic openness of goods, services, and foreign direct investment are all covered. An analysis of Central Asian economies is complicated by incompleteness and, sometimes, inconsistencies in these countries' social and economic data. To address this issue, this study relies on a mix of international and national data sources, which, taken together, provide a sufficiently coherent and realistic picture of developments in Central Asia. Appendix 1 contains a detailed discussion of data availability.

Endowed with natural resources and geographic uniqueness, Central Asia has much to gain from its economic connections with other regions. However, in order to maximize the development benefits of its geography and natural resources, Central Asia has to overcome several impediments, including those related to infrastructure, production technology, and market expansion overseas. Central Asia needs to make the most out of its networks of regional cooperation and institutions in order to propel the economic development of the region.

To reap the benefits of connecting the Central Asian republics with Asia and Europe in the coming decades, it is important to understand the region's overall development and macroeconomic conditions. Given that the economies of Central Asia have gone through structural adjustments and a revival of markets and production structure, an analysis of growth patterns and how they have changed over time will enable us to arrive at a policy strategy for sustainable development in Central Asia and greater economic integration with the major economic centers (Box 1.1).

Box 1.1 Economic Structure and Transition Record

Central Asian economies have come a long way since their independence from the former Soviet Union in the early 1990s. The overall success of transition in countries the region can be measured by a number of indicators, including the following.

Trade liberalization of imports and exports. Trade openness requires the removal of quantitative and administrative import and export restrictions. These include export tariffs; direct involvement in exports and imports by governments and state-owned trading companies; and non-uniform customs duties for non-agricultural goods and services.

Current account convertibility. Free movement of capital flows can be classified as full (complete compliance with Article VIII of the Articles of Agreement of the International Monetary Fund) or limited (restrictions on payments or transfers for current account transactions).

Controls on inward direct investment. Such controls are designed to influence foreign investment and technological transfers and include controls on foreign ownership and/or minimum capital requirements. In some cases, there may be no restrictions on inward foreign direct investment, except for arms production and military equipment.

Interest rate liberalization. This is required for the independent functioning of the capital markets. It may be full (banks are free to set deposit and lending rates); limited de facto (no legal restrictions on banks to set deposit and lending rates, but limitations arise from substantial market distortions, such as directed credits or poorly functioning or highly illiquid money or credit markets); or limited de jure (restrictions on banks' freedom to set interest rates through law, decree, or central bank regulation).

Exchange rate regime. Variants include a currency board, fixed, fixed with band, crawling peg, crawling peg with band, managed float, or floating.

Wage regulation. Restrictions or substantial taxes on the ability of some enterprises to adjust the average wage or wage bill upward.

Tradability of land. The purchase and sale of land can be full (no substantial restrictions on tradability of land rights beyond administrative requirements, no discrimination between domestic and foreign subjects);

continued on next page

Box 1.1 *continued*

full except for foreigners; limited de facto (substantial de facto limitations on tradability of land, for example, limited enforceability of land rights, a non-existent land market, or significant obstruction by government officials); limited de jure (legal restrictions on tradability of land rights); or none (land trade prohibited).

Capital adequacy ratio. Macro-prudential policy for the banking sector requires a capital adequacy ratio, the ratio of bank regulatory capital to risk-weighted assets. Regulatory capital includes paid-in capital, retentions, and some forms of subordinated debt.

Deposit insurance system. A measure to protect savings and to provide safety nets for the banking system, this can be full (deposits in all banks are covered by the formal deposit insurance scheme) or partial (some deposits are exempt).

Private pension funds. The availability of private pension funds helps to facilitate household savings and such funds can benefit long-term investment and development.

The following tables indicate how the five Central Asian countries perform against these transition development indicators. As can be seen, the tables indicate that the Central Asian economies have made significant progress in moving toward the market economy, although progress has not been uniform.

Table B1.1.1　Economic Development of Transitional Central Asia

Indicators of Economic Development in Transition		Kazakhstan	Kyrgyz Republic	Tajikistan	Turkmenistan	Uzbekistan
Liberalization and privatization	Current account convertibility	Full	Full	Full	Limited	Limited de facto
	Controls on inward direct investment	Yes	No	No	No	Yes
	Interest rate liberalization	Full	Full	Full	Limited de jure	Limited de jure
	Exchange rate regime	Pegged to US dollar	Managed float	Managed float	Fixed	Crawling peg
	Wage regulation	No	No	No	Yes	Yes
	Tradability of land	Full except for foreigners	Full except for foreigners	Limited de facto	Limited de jure	Limited de jure
Financial sector	Capital adequacy ratio	12%	12%	12%	10%	10%
	Deposit insurance system	Yes	Yes	Yes	No	Yes
	Private pension funds	Yes	Yes	No	No	No

Source: EBRD Transition Development Snapshots (http://www.ebrd.com/pages/research/economics/data/macro.shtml).

Central Asian countries are clearly pursuing different economic development paths. Large-scale privatization has already been achieved in the Kyrgyz Republic. However, there is room for further improvement in price liberalization in Uzbekistan. A common aspect of economic transition in Central Asia is the lack of progress on competition policy.

continued on next page

3

Box 1.1 *continued*

Table B1.1.2 Indicators of Transition in Central Asia

Country	Transition	1991	1995	2005	2012
Kazakhstan	Large-scale privatization	1.0	2.0	3.0	3.0
	Small-scale privatization	1.0	3.0	4.0	4.0
	Governance and enterprise restructuring	1.0	1.0	2.0	2.0
	Price liberalization	1.0	4.0	4.0	3.7
	Trade and foreign exchange system	1.0	3.0	3.7	3.7
	Competition policy	1.0	2.0	2.0	2.0
Kyrgyz Republic	Large-scale privatization	1.0	3.0	3.7	3.7
	Small-scale privatization	1.0	4.0	4.0	4.0
	Governance and enterprise restructuring	1.0	2.0	2.0	2.0
	Price liberalization	1.0	4.3	4.3	4.3
	Trade and foreign exchange system	1.0	4.0	4.3	4.3
	Competition policy	1.0	2.0	2.0	2.0
Tajikistan	Large-scale privatization	1.0	2.0	2.3	2.3
	Small-scale privatization	1.0	2.0	4.0	4.0
	Governance and enterprise restructuring	1.0	1.0	1.7	2.0
	Price liberalization	1.0	3.3	3.7	4.0
	Trade and foreign exchange system	1.0	2.0	3.3	3.3
	Competition policy	1.0	2.0	1.7	1.7
Turkmenistan	Large-scale privatization	1.0	1.0	1.0	1.0
	Small-scale privatization	1.0	1.7	2.0	2.3
	Governance and enterprise restructuring	1.0	1.0	1.0	1.0
	Price liberalization	1.0	2.7	2.7	3.0
	Trade and foreign exchange system	1.0	1.0	1.0	2.3
	Competition policy	1.0	1.0	1.0	1.0
Uzbekistan	Large-scale privatization	1.0	2.7	2.7	2.7
	Small-scale privatization	1.0	3.0	3.0	3.3
	Governance and enterprise restructuring	1.0	2.0	1.7	1.7
	Price liberalization	1.0	3.7	2.7	2.7
	Trade and foreign exchange system	1.0	2.0	2.0	1.7
	Competition policy	1.0	2.0	1.7	1.7

Note: The indicators range from 1 (no change from a centrally planned economy) to 4+ (standards of an industrialized market economy).
Source: EBRD Transition Indicators (http://www.ebrd.com/pages/research/economics/data/macro.shtml).

1.2   Pre- and Post-Transition Periods

Growth Patterns

Twenty years of transition in Central Asia have witnessed several major adjustments in the structure of economic development in the region. Following the breakup of the Soviet Union, the economies of Central Asia went through a dismal period, before a dramatic recovery in the late 1990s. Annual gross domestic product (GDP) during 1997–2012 grew remarkably in all countries of Central Asia (Figure 1.1A). According to the World Development Indicators, from 1997 to 2012 the average annual growth rate was 7.4% in Turkmenistan, 7.2% in Tajikistan, 6.7% in Kazakhstan, and 6.5% in Uzbekistan. The recovery has been extended to the present (ADB 2013a, 134–53).

It is important to understand the possible sources and potential consequences of Central Asia's recent growth performance. By and large, the five countries considered here can be divided into oil- and gas-exporting countries (Kazakhstan, Turkmenistan, and Uzbekistan) and non-oil-exporting countries (Kyrgyz Republic and Tajikistan).

High energy prices and investments in the oil and gas sector, including petrochemicals, have been the main growth drivers in Kazakhstan, Turkmenistan, and Uzbekistan. More specifically, growth performance in Kazakhstan is supported by investment in oil and natural gas, good macroeconomic management, and infrastructure investment, together with economic diversification into food processing, machinery, oil refinery, and chemicals. The economic performance of Turkmenistan is based on natural gas exports and foreign investment in textiles. Uzbekistan's economy has grown steadily from mining, manufacturing, and services.

The economic performance of the Kyrgyz Republic is largely due to minerals (gold) and services (especially re-exports and tourism), supported by migrant workers' remittances. For Tajikistan, agriculture, remittances, and foreign aid have provided the basis for growth. Workers' remittances play a huge role in Central Asia: the remittances to GDP ratios of the Kyrgyz Republic and Tajikistan are the highest in the world. Despite the recovery, however, the level of income in the non-oil-exporting group remains lower than in the oil- and gas-exporting countries, except Uzbekistan (Figures 1.1B and 1.1C).

Economic Performance by International Comparison

Since the force of globalization will influence the economic openness of Central Asia, it is crucial to evaluate how the region has performed relative to the rest of the world. Central Asia has done relatively well in the past 20 years; its GDP growth was below the global average during 1990–2000, but above it during 2001–2010 (Figure 1.2). Per capita incomes in Kazakhstan and Turkmenistan have risen to about US$10,000 in purchasing power parity (PPP) terms (Figure 1.3).

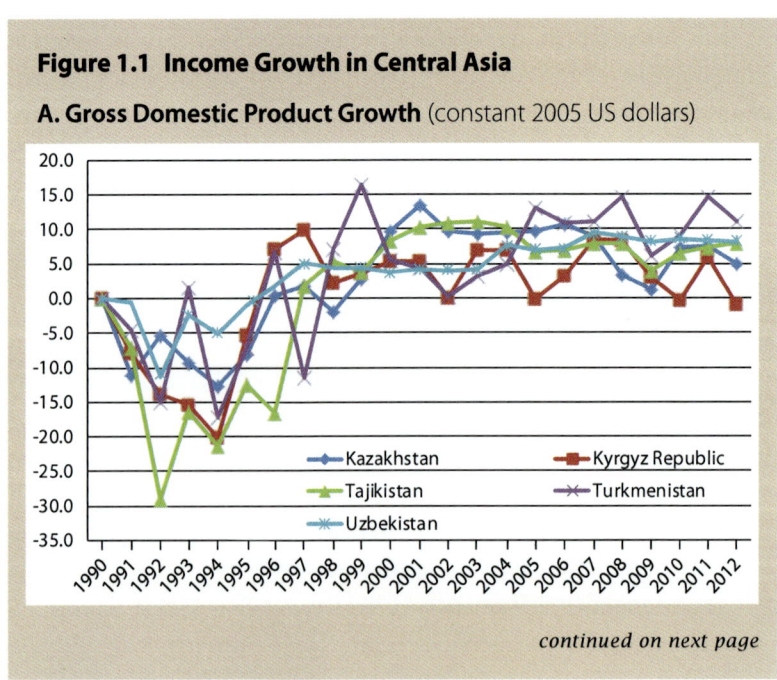

Figure 1.1 Income Growth in Central Asia

A. Gross Domestic Product Growth (constant 2005 US dollars)

continued on next page

Figure 1.1 *continued*

B. Per Capita Gross Domestic Product (purchasing power parity, constant 2005 international dollars)

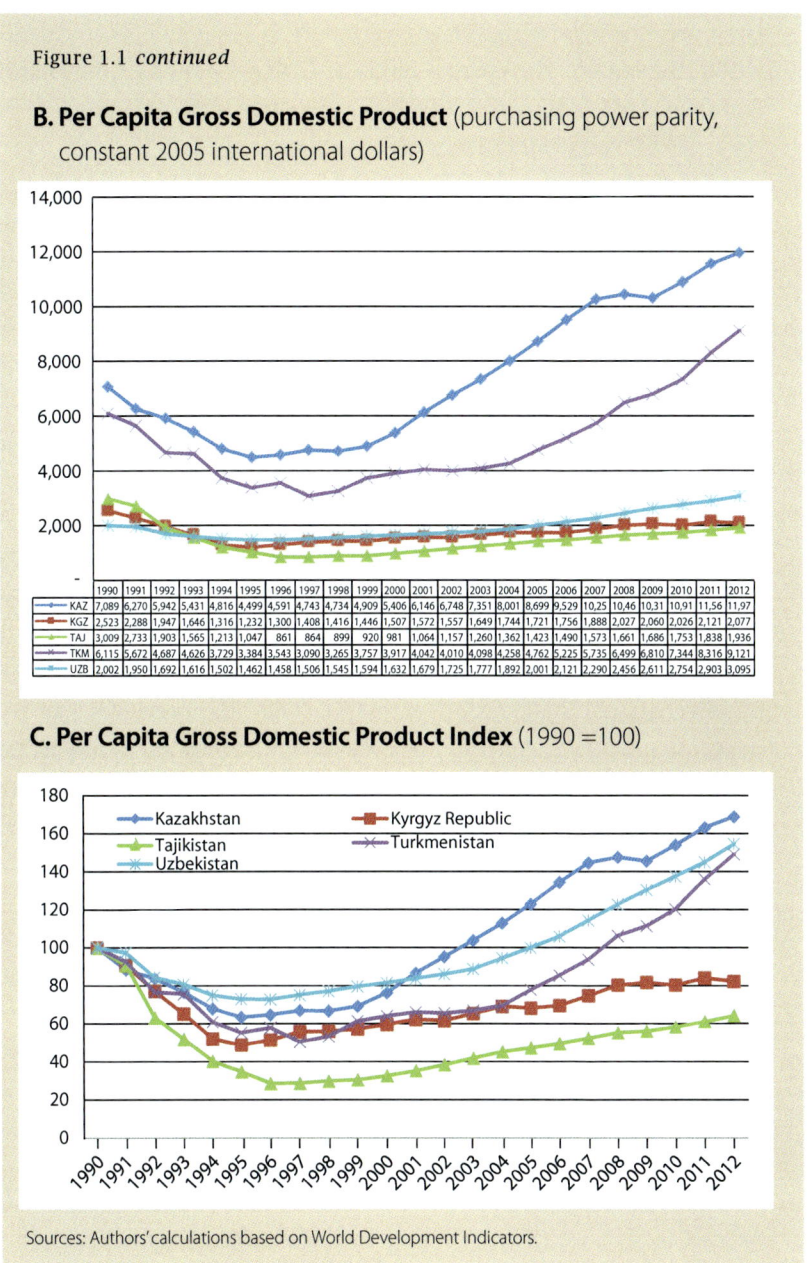

	1990	1991	1992	1993	1994	1995	1996	1997	1998	1999	2000	2001	2002	2003	2004	2005	2006	2007	2008	2009	2010	2011	2012
KAZ	7,089	6,270	5,942	5,431	4,816	4,499	4,591	4,743	4,734	4,909	5,406	6,146	6,748	7,351	8,001	8,699	9,529	10,25	10,46	10,31	10,91	11,56	11,97
KGZ	2,523	2,288	1,947	1,646	1,316	1,232	1,300	1,408	1,416	1,446	1,507	1,572	1,557	1,649	1,744	1,721	1,756	1,888	2,027	2,060	2,026	2,121	2,077
TAJ	3,009	2,733	1,903	1,565	1,213	1,047	861	864	899	920	981	1,064	1,157	1,260	1,362	1,423	1,490	1,573	1,661	1,686	1,753	1,838	1,936
TKM	6,115	5,672	4,687	4,626	3,729	3,384	3,543	3,090	3,265	3,757	3,917	4,042	4,010	4,098	4,258	4,762	5,225	5,735	6,499	6,810	7,344	8,316	9,121
UZB	2,002	1,950	1,692	1,616	1,502	1,462	1,458	1,506	1,545	1,594	1,632	1,679	1,725	1,777	1,892	2,001	2,121	2,290	2,456	2,611	2,754	2,903	3,095

C. Per Capita Gross Domestic Product Index (1990 =100)

Sources: Authors' calculations based on World Development Indicators.

However, there is a significant variation in economic performance within the region. The current levels of GDP per capita of the Kyrgyz Republic, Tajikistan, and Uzbekistan have not improved much from their pre-independence levels, standing below US$5,000 in PPP terms as of 2010. As a result, Kazakhstan and Turkmenistan are classified as upper middle-income countries; Uzbekistan as a lower-middle-income country; and the Kyrgyz Republic and Tajikistan remain in the group of low-income countries, although it is likely they will join the lower-middle-income category in the next few years.

In a cross-section of countries, the economic performance of countries in Central Asia follows a similar mean reversion pattern, as shown by the relationship between log GDP per capita in 1990 and log GDP per capita in 2010 (Figure 1.4). Over the past two decades, Kazakhstan and Turkmenistan have grown significantly by international standards, whereas the economic performance of the Kyrgyz Republic, Tajikistan, and Uzbekistan is comparable with those of other low- and middle-income countries. The levels of poverty in some countries of Central Asia[1] have remained at alarming levels by international standards (Figure 1.5). While the percentage of the population below the poverty line has dropped over the years, in the Kyrgyz Republic and Tajikistan, 35%–50% of the population remains below the national poverty line. Only Kazakhstan has managed to reduce poverty significantly; from more than 40% to 4% of the population.

Since autarky is no longer an option, sequencing trade and investment connectivity with rest of the world, especially further eastward to Asia and westward to Europe, should offer the countries of Central Asia new sustainable growth opportunities. They will need both to specialize in their core competences and to diversify and integrate into global value chains of production if they are to take advantage of these.

To understand growth performance across countries in Central Asia, it is also worth considering several macroeconomic indicators (Table 1.1). Over the past decade, domestic savings as a percentage of GDP have increased, but there is room for further growth, which should help provide a basis for domestic investment. In addition,

---

[1]   There are no recent poverty data for Turkmenistan and Uzbekistan.

Figure 1.2 Income Growth by International Comparison

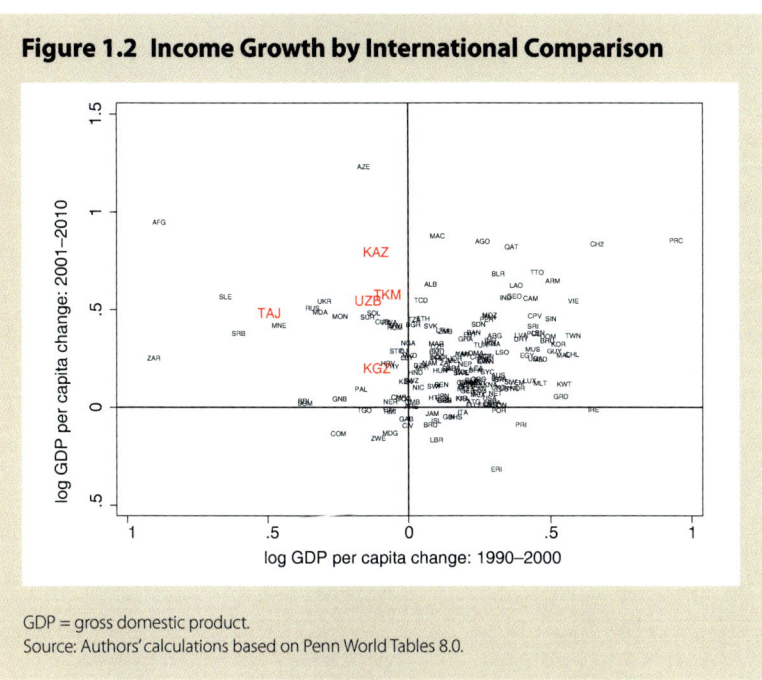

GDP = gross domestic product.
Source: Authors' calculations based on Penn World Tables 8.0.

Figure 1.3 Income Level of Central Asia (PPP converted at 2005 constant prices)

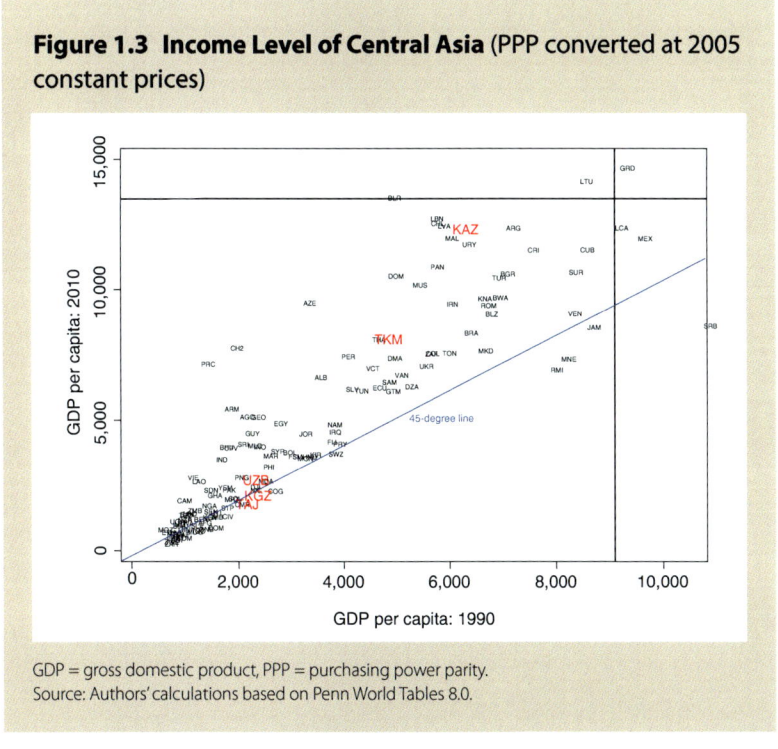

GDP = gross domestic product, PPP = purchasing power parity.
Source: Authors' calculations based on Penn World Tables 8.0.

Figure 1.4 Income Level by International Comparison

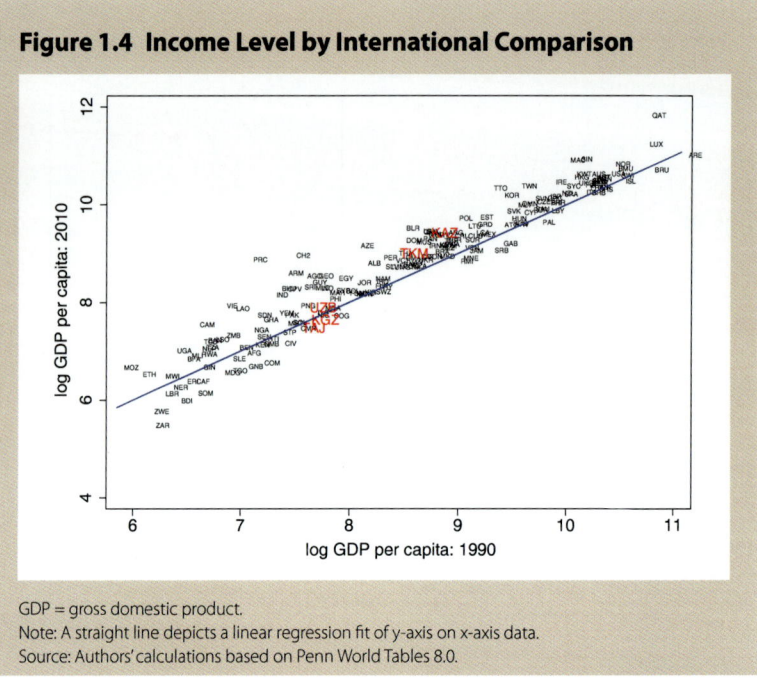

GDP = gross domestic product.
Note: A straight line depicts a linear regression fit of y-axis on x-axis data.
Source: Authors' calculations based on Penn World Tables 8.0.

Figure 1.5 Poverty Headcount by International Comparison (%)

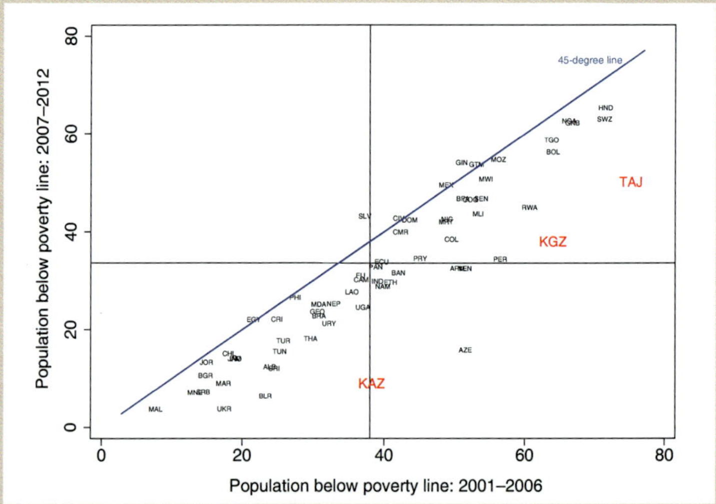

GDP = gross domestic product, PPP = purchasing power parity.
Note: In percent of population; a straight-diagonal line depicts 45 degrees. Inter-country comparisons based on national poverty lines are subject to data collection methods; definitions and values of national poverty lines are different across countries. In Kazakhstan, the poverty line is set at US$4.2/day PPP; in the Kyrgyz Republic it is US$3.1/day PPP; and in Tajikistan it is US$3.0/day PPP.
Source: Authors' calculations based on World Development Indicators.

Table 1.1 Macroeconomic Indicators of Central Asia (%)

Macroeconomic Indicators	Kazakhstan		Kyrgyz Republic		Tajikistan		Turkmenistan		Uzbekistan	
	2003	2012	2003	2012	2003	2012	2003	2012	2003	2012
Domestic savings/GDP	34.3	42.6	5.3	..	9.3	..	25.4	..	26.9	32.0
Domestic investment/GDP	25.7	23.3	11.8	32.4	10.0	..	31.1	..	20.2	28.9
Government taxes/GDP	20.5	13.6	14.2	21.0	15.0	19.9	18.3	..	22.4	20.3
Budget balance/GDP	−0.9	−2.9	−0.8	−6.6	1.1	−3.1	−0.1	6.0	−1.3	0.4
Consumer price inflation (annual)	6.4	5.1	3.1	2.8	13.7	6.4	5.6	5.3	10.3	7.2
International reserves/GDP	16.1	14.0	20.8	31.9	7.6	8.2	23.4	..	16.3	..

.. = not available, GDP = gross domestic product.
Source: Authors' calculations based on ADB (2013c).

an improvement in the tax base of Central Asian governments, now standing at 14%–22% of GDP, could also strengthen the budget balance positions, which have been in deficit throughout this 10-year period. A strong fiscal position, together with active currency management and more ample international reserves (currently 16%–23% of GDP), should also help rein in high inflation and stabilize prices in comparison with those in other regions.

1.3   Production Structure in Transition

While there are many reasons to be positive about the prospects for Central Asia, questions remain over whether economic growth is too dependent on natural resource extraction, exports of low-end manufactures, and agricultural products with fluctuating terms of trade (Dowling and Wignaraja 2006a). In addition, over the past 10 years, the services sector in Central Asia, supported by workers' remittances, has grown rapidly in some countries, implying that their economic interdependence with other countries has become

11

more important and concentrated. Oil and natural resources will eventually be exhausted so countries need to determine the degree of diversification in product space (number of products, variety of products, and quality of products) and market destinations (Hamilton 2013, 29–63).

In terms of production structure, the transition period in Central Asia that started in 1989–1991 was followed by the most active phase of transition during 1991–1999 as countries moved away from the Soviet model of economic development. Key features of the economies of countries of Central Asia were inherited from its links with the production structure of the former Soviet Union; in the early periods of transition, the product space and market destinations of Central Asia were small and confined to products mostly supplied to the Russian Federation and other former Soviet republics.

Since the early 1990s, adjustments to their production structure have varied across countries in terms of the value added across sectors, and the size of exports and imports over the years. Previous studies (Dowling and Wignaraja 2006a, 2006b) have pointed to fundamental differences between the oil and gas exporters (Kazakhstan, Turkmenistan, and Uzbekistan) and the two countries that do not export oil (Kyrgyz Republic and Tajikistan). Throughout the past two decades, economic growth in the region has been driven primarily by the oil and gas sectors in Kazakhstan and Turkmenistan, although there have also been some shifts toward industrial goods and minerals, as well as services, away from agriculture across Central Asian countries (Table 1.2).

The services sector has become an important part of production in Central Asia and already accounts for about the half of value added of GDP. While the value added from the services sector has always been large in Kazakhstan, services have recently expanded considerably in the other four countries as well. Further improvements to the services sector, particularly to banking and financial systems, as well as reductions in the regulatory barriers that hinder moves toward a market-based economy, should support a further expansion of services and increase the size of domestic markets and consumption in Central Asia.

Of the non-oil-exporting economies, the share of industry in GDP in the Kyrgyz Republic has grown, but in Tajikistan it has declined,

Table 1.2 Production Structure and International Trade of Central Asia

Country	Industry Value-Added (% of GDP)			Services Value-Added (% of GDP)			Agriculture Value-Added (% of GDP)			GDP (US$ billion)	Exports (US$ billion)	Imports (US$ billion)
	1995	2005	2012	1995	2005	2012	1995	2005	2012	2012	2012	2012
Oil and Gas Exporters												
Kazakhstan	31.2	39.2	39.2	56.0	54.2	56.3	12.8	6.6	4.5	202.7	92.3	44.9
Turkmenistan	65.3	37.6	48.4	17.9	43.6	37.0	16.9	18.8	14.5	33.7	20.0	14.1
Uzbekistan	27.8	28.8	33.4	39.8	43.1	46.8	32.4	28.1	19.8	50.9	14.3	12.0
Non-Oil Exporters												
Kyrgyz Republic	19.4	22.0	28.2	37.5	46.7	53.1	43.1	31.3	18.7	6.5	1.9	5.4
Tajikistan	36.5	30.7	27.9	27.6	45.6	50.3	35.9	23.8	21.8	7.6	1.4	3.8

GDP = gross domestic product.
Source: Authors' calculations based on ADB (2013c).

largely because of the size of its services sector. Industrial recovery in Central Asia is closely linked to the amount of international trade countries engage in, which has become quite large relative to the size of GDP. Both oil and gas exporters and non-oil-exporting countries have had respectable exports of manufactured goods compared with countries at a similar stage of development. However, the size of manufactured exports is subject to the definition. If gold is included in the Kyrgyz Republic (gold refining is part of manufacturing, not mining), manufactured exports are more than half of total exports of goods. On the other hand, if gold is excluded—and aluminum in Tajikistan, and ferrous and non-ferrous metals in Kazakhstan and Uzbekistan are also excluded—manufacturing exports are much smaller. The structure of manufacturing also varies across countries. Textile and related products made up most of the manufactured exports of Turkmenistan, the Kyrgyz Republic, and Uzbekistan. Ferrous and non-ferrous metals and non-metallic minerals account for the majority of manufactured exports in Kazakhstan, the Kyrgyz Republic, Tajikistan, and Uzbekistan. Uzbekistan has also become a large exporter of automobiles in recent years. Chapter 2 will discuss the composition of international trade in more detail.

Over the past two decades, there have also been subtle changes in the factors of production and factor incomes, notably the size of the labor force, unemployment, and workers' remittances (Table 1.3). Until the early 2000s, agriculture was the major driver of growth in non-oil-exporting countries, particularly the Kyrgyz Republic and Uzbekistan. This was because of generally favorable weather conditions, high world prices for cotton and wheat, and agricultural reforms. Some productivity gains were also achieved in the collective farms producing cotton and wheat. However, trade volatility and fluctuations in world prices have led to a move over recent years toward higher value-added manufacturing and service sectors. As a result, workers have left agriculture and moved from rural to urban areas.

Unemployment remains a problem in Kazakhstan and the Kyrgyz Republic. While unemployment rates appear relatively low in Uzbekistan and Tajikistan, this may reflect differences in the measurements of unemployment rate and labor force participation rate across countries. More evidence is needed from the labor market to understand why the level of poverty has not declined significantly in Central Asia after the two decades of transition. A detailed analysis of the labor market should reveal underlying factors of poverty in Central Asia that can be traced back to the early 1990s, including the breakdown of production and distribution networks, the collapse of social security systems, high inflation caused by disruptions in the production of key goods, loss of control over the money supply, civil strife in several countries, and migration of skilled Russian workers.

Workers' remittances have increased in all countries, although the data are scarce and in some cases inconsistent and unreliable. Workers' remittances have become particularly important since the early 2000s in the Kyrgyz Republic and Tajikistan, with most migrant workers from these economies entering the labor markets of the Russian Federation or those of Asian neighbors. Despite this, unemployment rates in the Kyrgyz Republic remain significant. Data from the National Statistical Committee show that the highest unemployment rate (based on International Labour Organization definitions) was 12.5% in 2002. From 2004 to 2012, the rate fluctuated from 8.1% to 8.5%. While Kazakhstan has not been so reliant on workers' remittances, and has cut its unemployment rate by almost half from the late 1990s, unemployment is still high. Unemployment and poverty are particularly pronounced in the Fergana Valley and border regions of Uzbekistan, the Kyrgyz Republic, and Tajikistan.

Table 1.3 Labor Force, Income from Remittances, and Unemployment

| Country | Population (million) | | Labor Force (million) | | Unemployment Rate (%) | | Remittances | |
	1995	2011	1995	2011	1995	2011	Cumulative, 2002–2012 (US$ million)	2012 (% of GDP)
Oil and Gas Exporters								
Kazakhstan	15.8	16.6	7.4	8.8	11.0	5.4	1,707.2	0.1
Turkmenistan	4.2	5.1	1.9	..	..	..	..	..
Uzbekistan	22.7	29.3	8.5	12.5	0.3	0.1	..	..
Non-Oil Exporters								
Kyrgyz Republic	4.5	5.5	1.7	2.5	5.7	8.5	9,005.4	31.3
Tajikistan	5.7	7.8	1.9	2.3	2.0	1.0	16,672.8	44.2

.. = not available, GDP = gross domestic product.
Note: Unemployment rates are based on different definitions. For Kazakhstan and the Kyrgyz Republic, data are based on the International Labour Organization's definition of unemployment. In the other three countries, which do not have labor force surveys, these are officially registered unemployment rates.
Sources: Authors' calculations based on ADB (2013c).

1.4   Conclusions

Initial conditions have played an important role in shaping the drivers of and impediments to economic development in Central Asia. The location of industrial sites, concentrations of output and production, and infrastructure connectivity in the region were, in the main, inherited from the pre-transition period. The transition to market-oriented economies requires a major reallocation of resources and significant efforts to ensure they are efficiently used. Initial conditions have played an important role in shaping the drivers of and impediments to economic development in Central Asia. The location of industrial sites, concentrations of output and production, and infrastructure connectivity in the region were, in the main, inherited from the pre-transition period. The transition to market-oriented economies requires a major reallocation of resources and significant efforts to ensure they are efficiently used.

Previous studies have pointed to several factors contributing to growth in Central Asia, including exports of minerals and energy-related products; industrialization, technology transfers, and job creation based on foreign direct investment; and the supportive role of macroeconomic management and political stability promoted by national governments (Dowling and Wignaraja 2006b). These factors will continue to be important for Central Asia in coming years.

While the extraction of natural resources has provided a basis for economic development in most parts of the region, deposits of oil, gas, and minerals will be exhausted one day, and not all Central Asian countries are equally well endowed with such resources. Growth in high value-added manufacturing needs to be strengthened, together with the services sector. The sustainability of economic development in Central Asia will depend on trade and financial integration and investment in infrastructure, transportation, trade facilitation, and institutional capacity. These issues will be taken up in the following chapters.

Central Asian economies are small open economies and need to put in place macro-prudential policies that take into account externalities such as currency depreciation and potential competitive devaluations by major trading partners and other economies supplying similar commodities, which could have significant effects on cross-border flows of trade and foreign investment. To offset the negative impact of such cyclical fluctuations, policy makers need to actively manage stabilization funds and employ counter-cyclical policy tools (Gill et al. 2014, 28–29).

2. Trade Ties between Central Asia and Economic Centers

2.1　Introduction

This chapter focuses on patterns of trade and possible gains and costs of further trade integration. Patterns of trade are considered in terms of the geography of trading partners, together with factor endowment, technology of production, and factor proportions in export and import patterns. The diversification of trading partners and products are then analyzed from intensive (volume and values of trade) and extensive (number of trading partners and number of trading products) margins, as well as the role of exporting and non-exporting firms. Gains, costs, and distributional conflicts are then discussed.

There are lessons to be learned from the existing cross-border trade of Central Asia with major economic centers and other regions. The features of exports, imports, and total trade of Central Asia, together with its trading relationships, product composition, proximity to trading partners, industry concentration, and supporting factors, need to be examined in order to understand Central Asia's potential future trade ties.

An examination of existing trade patterns will provide a better understanding of product space and market destinations, and of ways to improve them. This should also help Central Asia to reap gains from trade and to minimize costs. There are several policy challenges that should be considered, including economic diversification and moving production chains upscale and linking to factories in Asia to create more value-added and increase employment.

In order for Central Asia to maximize benefits from further trade integration, developments such as the customs union between Belarus, Kazakhstan, and the Russian Federation, and World Trade Organization (WTO) accession status of the five countries will play an important role. A better understanding of trade costs and the institutional factors that influence international trade is also important (Helpman 2011, 126–65). Such trade costs include not only transportation costs and those related to trade barriers, but also trade facilitation and institutions (see Box 2.1 for tariff protection in Central Asia). They are particularly important for Central Asian economies given their geography and development in the transition period. This chapter focuses on the patterns of trade and potential gains and costs, Chapter 4 will discuss policy issues, regional cooperation, and institutional factors.

Box 2.1   Tariff Protection in Central Asia

Comprehensive data on tariff rates are difficult to come by for developing and transition economies. This is clearly the case for Central Asia. The lack of data makes it difficult not only to understand the patterns of protection in the region, but also to analyze in detail the welfare implications of tariff reductions and free trade agreements. The lack of information needed to understand and fully assess the costs and benefits of the customs union of Belarus, Kazakhstan, and the Russian Federation is a case in point. Despite these constraints, existing data provide a rough picture of tariff protection in Central Asia. The level of protection for the agricultural sector is similar throughout the region, whereas there are differences in the level of protection provided to industrial sectors.

Table B2.1.1 Most Favored Nation (MFN) Tariffs (%)

Country	Tariff Year	Simple Average			Trade Weighted Average		
		Total trade	Agricultural	Industrial	Total trade	Agricultural	Industrial
Kazakhstan	2012	9.5	13.4	8.8	9.4	19.5	8.2
Kyrgyz Republic	2012	4.6	7.4	4.2	3.8	5.5	3.4
Tajikistan	2012	7.8	10.8	7.3	7.2	5.4	8.1
Turkmenistan	2002	5.1	8.3	4.2	2.9	12.6	1.1
Uzbekistan	2012	15.4	19.2	14.9	10.9	13.7	9.6

Source: World Trade Organization (http://www.wto.org), World Databank (http://databank.worldbank.org/data/home.aspx).

2.2   Patterns of Trade

Trade in Goods

While economic openness will be important in Central Asia for years to come, it is likely to develop unevenly across countries in the region. Tajikistan and Turkmenistan are currently the most open economies, measured by the level of exports and imports as a percentage of GDP (Figure 2.1). Since historical evidence of the association between growth and openness has been inconclusive (Lee, Ricci, and Rigobon 2004), this implies that the experiences and prospects of Central Asia on economic connectivity may also be unique in terms of the costs and benefits that will be faced by the region. There will be gainers and losers from more economic integration, but efforts need to be made to maximize the potential gains of all stakeholders in an expansion of economic connectivity.

External trade in goods has generally improved for countries in Central Asia over the past 10 years (Table 2.1). In Kazakhstan, exports

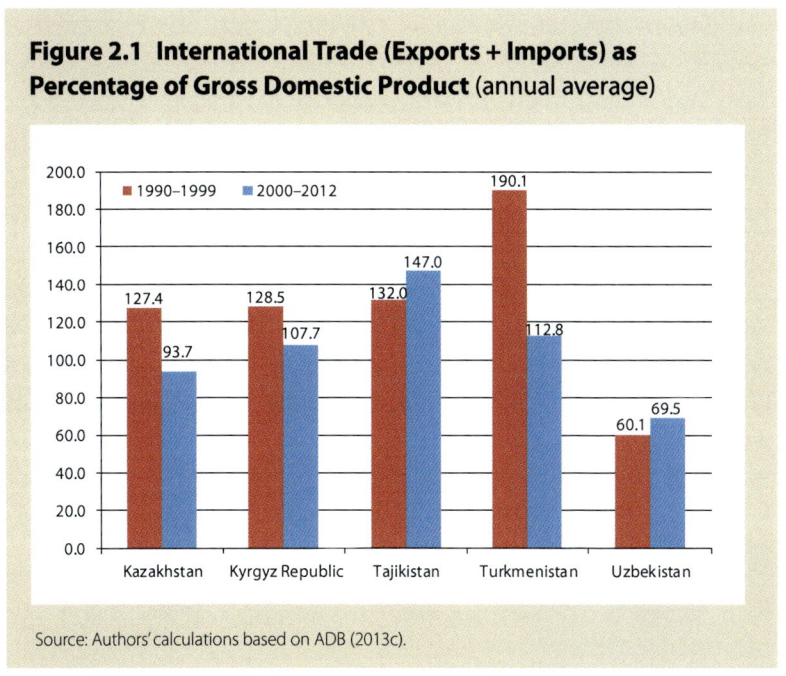

Figure 2.1   International Trade (Exports + Imports) as Percentage of Gross Domestic Product (annual average)

Source: Authors' calculations based on ADB (2013c).

Table 2.1 Balance of Payments Current Account in Central Asia (US$ billion)

Country		Goods		Services and Income		Current Transfers	
		Exports	Imports	Credit	Debit	Credit	Debit
Oil and Gas Exporters							
Kazakhstan	2003	13.2	9.6	2.0	5.8	0.3	0.4
	2012	92.1	47.4	6.8	42.8	2.6	3.6
Turkmenistan	2003	3.5	2.6	..	..	..	..
	2012	19.9	13.4	..	..	..	..
Uzbekistan	2003	3.2	2.4	..	..	..	..
	2012	14.6	11.0	..	..	..	..
Non-Oil Exporters							
Kyrgyz Republic	2003	0.6	0.7	0.2	0.2	0.2	0.01
	2012	2.0	5.0	1.2	1.6	2.3	0.3
Tajikistan	2003	0.9	1.0	0.1	0.2	0.3	0.1
	2012	0.8	4.4	0.9	1.0	3.7	0.3

.. = not available.
Source: Authors' calculations based on ADB (2013c).

and imports have grown rapidly and the country has registered an overall trade surplus over the past decade. Strong export earnings have facilitated import growth, primarily of consumer goods, and fueled economic growth and investments in goods related to major oil and natural gas. Exports of the Kyrgyz Republic, Tajikistan, and Uzbekistan have all increased in nominal US dollar terms, although if one accounts for the real purchasing power of the US dollar, Tajikistan experienced a decrease in its real exports and the Kyrgyz Republic had almost no growth. For these two countries, export growth has been offset by a larger increase in imports, resulting in a deterioration of trade balances. Meeting needs for infrastructure investment and demands for consumer goods may prove a challenge for non-oil-exporting economies if they continue to rely on export revenues from low-end manufactures, textiles, and workers' remittances to finance their imports.

Trade in Services

Trade in services has grown substantially in Central Asia. The expansion of the financial sector in Kazakhstan and the size of remittance incomes for the Kyrgyz Republic and Tajikistan have contributed to this trend in recent years. While the data on trade in services are scattered and not as well classified in comparison to data on trade in goods, they suggest that trade in services in Central Asia has more than doubled in the last decade (Table 2.2). Financial services, telecommunications, real estate, and tourism will become ever more important, and greater financial deepening, boosted by higher domestic demand for credit, will help to expand and open up the banking and financial sector. Investment in infrastructure, including further upgrading of telecommunications and business services, will help support production, employment, and international trade in the services sector (see Box 2.2 for tourism in Central Asia).

Table 2.2 Trade in Services in Central Asia (US$ billion)

Country	Period	Exports	Imports	Total Trade
Kazakhstan	2000–2006	12.6	33.1	45.8
	2007–2012	25.9	67.8	93.8
Kyrgyz Republic	2000–2006	1.3	1.6	2.8
	2007–2012	5.5	6.1	11.5
Tajikistan	2000–2006	0.6	1.1	1.6
	2007–2012	2.2	3.5	5.8
Turkmenistan	2000–2006	..	..	..
	2007–2012	..	..	..
Uzbekistan	2000–2006	..	..	..
	2007–2012	6.3	2.1	8.4

.. = not available.
Note: Data were derived from World Trade Organization (WTO) Trade in Commercial Services. Services items correspond to the code number of S200 and were cross-checked with United Nations (UN) data (including those in the Extended Balance of Payments Services Classification [EBOPS], UN Service Trade Statistics Database Classification); services trade exclude EBOPS memorandum items and EBOPS supplementary items (Total EBOPS corresponds to a code number of 200). The discrepancy in the data on trade in services between WTO and UN service trade is because EBOPS does not include trade flows on supplementary and memorandum items; hence, the services flows in WTO data tend to be larger than those in UN services trade data.
Source: Authors' calculations based on WTO Trade in Commercial Services.

Box 2.2 Tourism: Potential and Pitfalls

Tourism constitutes an important and steadily growing part of the world economy's trade in services. According to the World Tourism Organization's World Tourism Barometer report (April 2014), the number of total international tourist visits in 2013 increased to 52 million people in 2012 total (UNWTO 2014). Tourism's contribution to total export earnings was US$1.4 trillion, the receipts earned by destinations increased by 5% over the previous year, reaching US$1,159 billion worldwide.

In relative terms, Asia and the Pacific recorded the largest increase in total tourism receipts by destination in 2013 (8%), followed by the Americas (6%) and Europe (4%).

Tourism can be categorized by its purposes into: recreational tourism, seasonal tourism (Easter, Christmas), and heritage tourism. The latter type represents a complex notion that is characterized by the existence of historical architecture or artifacts.

In this respect, Central Asian countries, which possess the diverse inheritance of the Great Silk Road, have vast opportunities that are still to be fully realized. According to World Development Indicators, the number of tourist arrivals in the Kyrgyz Republic increased from 1.4 million in 2009 to 2.4 million in 2012, while arrivals in Kazakhstan increased from 2.9 million to 4.8 million over the same period. These figures look good in relative terms and there is huge potential for growth in absolute terms: by comparison, in 2012 Egypt received 11 million arrivals and Mexico 23 million.

How can countries in Central Asia increase the number of tourist arrivals? Tourism has been described as an asymmetric market (Cohen 1979; Smeral 1993). Generally, due to the existence of imperfect information, "sellers" of a product know its real characteristics and value while potential "buyers" do not. With regard to Central Asia, both sides have asymmetric information.

For example, Samarkand, which was established as Afrasiab in the 7th century BCE and currently contains relics of the most important stages of the political, economic, and cultural life of Central Asia from the 13th century to the present, is located in Uzbekistan. A unique feature of the city is that the footprints of previous historical phases do not appear in chronological order but rather are ingrained alongside each other. As a result, one can observe the site of the ancient city of Afrasiab, which was an important part of Alexander the Great's Empire in 4th century BCE, along with remnants of the cultural and scientific life of the medieval city of the Temurid epoch of the 14th and 15th centuries CE, illustrated in the architectural ensembles of Registan Square and the remains of Ulughbek's Observatory. The 19th and 20th century expansions in the European style built during the Russian and Soviet periods conclude the story.

Central Asia needs to learn from such famous sites as the Coliseum in Rome, Stonehenge in the United Kingdom, and the Pyramid of Khufu at Giza in Egypt. These provide good examples of well-preserved and excellently marketed heritage tourism destinations.

The transition countries in Asia should first identify and evaluate the full potential of their tourism industries. This should be followed by active government policies oriented toward broader promotion of that potential in abroad as well as radically upgraded marketing strategies and services by private companies involved

continued on next page

Box 2.2 *continued*

in tourism. Although the development of the Internet has contributed a lot to the elimination of asymmetric information, systematic work to ensure a consistent supply of customized and accurate information is vital to the growth of tourism services (Schwabe, Novak, and Aggeler 2008).

Finally, the positive effects from the measures mentioned above can only be achieved by the preliminary provision of a hard platform for mobility in general (Seetanah et al. 2011), that is, the countries need to establish an efficient and reliable infrastructure base if guests are to be able move between sites (Gunn 1988; Inskeep 1991).

Table B2.2.1 Exports of Tourism Services in Central Asia, 2013

	US$ million	Percentage of Total Exports of Goods and Services
Kazakhstan	1,460	1.6
Kyrgyz Republic	530	17.1
Tajikistan	3	0.2
Uzbekistan	615	4.1

Note: No data for Turkmenistan.
Sources: National banks of Kazakhstan, the Kyrgyz Republic, and Tajikistan; State Committee on Statistics of Uzbekistan.

Geography of Trading Partners

The main impediments to international trade are long distances from trading partners and related costs of transportation and trade facilitation. Ongoing development projects to establish economic corridors have been trying to overcome these barriers for Central Asia (Figure 2.2). The relationship between the size of Central Asia's bilateral trade and its distance from its trading partners can be seen in the data over the past two decades (Figure 2.3). The role of economic corridors and infrastructure will be discussed in more detail in Section 4.4.

The trade–distance nexus of Central Asia is largely expected, given the region's geography and history of bilateral trade relationships with a small number of trading partners. After the breakup of the Soviet Union in the early 1990s, Central Asia's bilateral trade remained

Figure 2.2 Economic Corridors of Central Asia

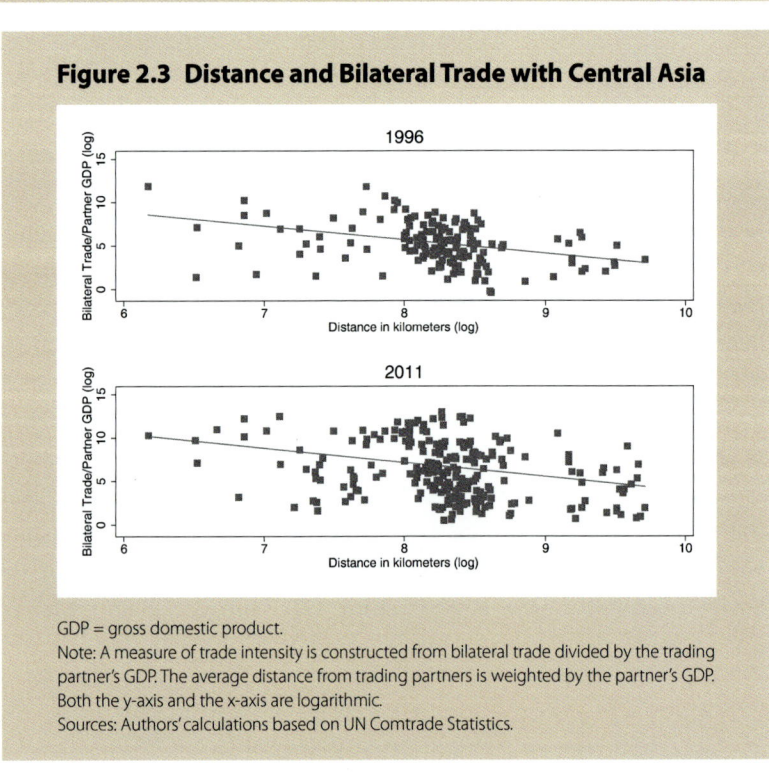

Source: CAREC (2012).

Figure 2.3 Distance and Bilateral Trade with Central Asia

GDP = gross domestic product.
Note: A measure of trade intensity is constructed from bilateral trade divided by the trading partner's GDP. The average distance from trading partners is weighted by the partner's GDP. Both the y-axis and the x-axis are logarithmic.
Sources: Authors' calculations based on UN Comtrade Statistics.

concentrated on the Russian Federation and the European Union. Only in the past decade has trade between Central Asia and East Asia (People's Republic of China [PRC], Japan, and Republic of Korea) started to gain significance, although it is still smaller than trade with the European Union (Table 2.3).

Table 2.3 Merchandise Trade between Central Asia and Economic Centers

Country	Economic Centers	Period	Cumulative Exports		Cumulative Imports		Cumulative Total Trade	
			US$ billion	2000s/1990s ratio	US$ billion	2000s/1990s ratio	US$ billion	2000s/1990s ratio
Kazakhstan	ASEAN	1992–1999	0.40		0.07		0.47	
		2000–2012	0.99	2.5	2.15	28.8	3.15	6.6
	South Asia	1992–1999	0.15		0.19		0.34	
		2000–2012	3.75	24.7	2.07	10.7	5.82	16.9
	PRC, Japan, and Rep. of Korea	1992–1999	2.98		1.16		4.15	
		2000–2012	74.44	25.0	45.21	38.8	119.64	28.8
	United States	1992–1999	0.53		1.15		1.68	
		2000–2012	6.76	12.7	13.22	11.5	19.98	11.9
	Russian Federation	1992–1999	11.33		10.55		21.88	
		2000–2012	39.49	3.5	85.42	8.1	124.87	5.7
	European Union	1992–1999	16.49		12.64		29.12	
		2000–2012	355.56	21.6	120.82	9.6	476.33	16.4
Kyrgyz Republic	ASEAN	1992–1999	0.00		0.00		0.01	
		2000–2012	0.02	16.0	0.07	14.8	0.09	15.6
	South Asia	1992–1999	0.03		0.12		0.15	
		2000–2012	0.51	15.1	0.22	1.9	0.73	4.9
	PRC, Japan, and Rep. of Korea	1992–1999	0.26		0.23		0.49	
		2000–2012	0.63	2.4	23.42	101.5	24.05	49.0
	United States	1992–1999	0.06		0.29		0.34	
		2000–2012	0.10	1.7	1.02	3.6	1.12	3.2
	Russian Federation	1992–1999	0.77		1.18		1.95	
		2000–2012	2.38	3.1	9.39	7.9	11.76	6.0
	European Union	1992–1999	2.45		2.69		5.14	
		2000–2012	7.46	3.1	12.83	4.8	20.28	3.9

continued on next page

Table 2.3 *continued*

Country	Economic Centers	Period	Cumulative Exports		Cumulative Imports		Cumulative Total Trade	
			US$ billion	2000s/1990s ratio	US$ billion	2000s/1990s ratio	US$ billion	2000s/1990s ratio
Tajikistan	ASEAN	1992–1999	0.01		0.00		0.01	
		2000–2012	0.03	3.7	0.03	21.1	0.06	6.4
	South Asia	1992–1999	0.01		0.02		0.03	
		2000–2012	0.45	41.8	0.59	27.4	1.04	32.2
	PRC, Japan, and Rep. of Korea	1992–1999	0.08		0.03		0.11	
		2000–2012	1.17	14.1	5.72	202.1	6.88	62.0
	United States	1992–1999	0.08		0.13		0.21	
		2000–2012	0.04	0.6	0.63	4.9	0.67	3.3
	Russian Federation	1992–1999	0.51		0.66		1.17	
		2000–2012	1.26	2.5	6.53	9.8	7.79	6.6
	European Union	1992–1999	3.78		3.91		7.67	
		2000–2012	10.22	2.7	13.85	3.5	24.06	3.1
Turkmenistan	ASEAN	1992–1999	0.02		0.00		0.03	
		2000–2012	0.02	1.1	0.46	95.3	0.48	18.7
	South Asia	1992–1999	0.18		0.08		0.26	
		2000–2012	2.47	13.6	0.43	5.7	2.90	11.3
	PRC, Japan, and Rep. of Korea	1992–1999	0.20		0.23		0.43	
		2000–2012	12.68	63.2	7.34	32.6	20.01	47.0
	United States	1992–1999	0.09		0.91		1.01	
		2000–2012	1.04	11.3	1.99	2.2	3.04	3.0
	Russian Federation	1992–1999	0.28		0.84		1.12	
		2000–2012	2.04	7.2	7.75	9.3	9.78	8.7
	European Union	1992–1999	5.74		5.77		11.51	
		2000–2012	46.92	8.2	35.72	6.2	82.63	7.2

continued on next page

Table 2.3 *continued*

Country	Economic Centers	Period	Cumulative Exports US$ billion	Cumulative Exports 2000s/1990s ratio	Cumulative Imports US$ billion	Cumulative Imports 2000s/1990s ratio	Cumulative Total Trade US$ billion	Cumulative Total Trade 2000s/1990s ratio
Uzbekistan	ASEAN	1992–1999	0.24		0.09		0.33	
		2000–2012	0.31	1.3	0.48	5.3	0.80	2.4
	South Asia	1992–1999	0.14		0.26		0.40	
		2000–2012	3.46	24.5	0.63	2.4	4.09	10.1
	PRC, Japan, and Rep. of Korea	1992–1999	0.83		0.89		1.73	
		2000–2012	6.83	8.2	11.01	12.3	17.85	10.3
	United States	1992–1999	0.27		1.50		1.76	
		2000–2012	1.18	4.4	2.24	1.5	3.42	1.9
	Russian Federation	1992–1999	4.00		4.77		8.77	
		2000–2012	10.82	2.7	17.21	3.6	28.04	3.2
	European Union	1992–1999	9.63		13.95		21.68	
		2000–2012	31.53	3.3	46.31	3.3	77.84	3.6

ASEAN = Association of Southeast Asian Nations, PRC = People's Republic of China.
Source: Authors' calculations based on UN Comtrade Statistics.

Comparative Advantage: Endowment, Technology, and Factor Proportions

To understand Central Asia's trade links, it is useful to examine the region's comparative advantage, although the unbundling of global trade, which is now driven by global value chains, means that comparative advantage can vary over time and become more regional, rather than country-specific. Comparative advantage also tends to vary across product space, implying the potential advantage of building networks in international trade and the benefits of joining the global value chains.

Patterns of revealed comparative advantage do not proceed evenly across product categories or over time for Central Asia (Figure 2.4).[2] The region's reliance on a few homogeneous commodities, e.g., oil, gas, minerals, and natural resource exports, indicates the importance for Central Asia of further developing high value-added manufacturing sectors (i.e., differentiated products) and networks in international trade (Rauch 1999).

Figure 2.4 Revealed Comparative Advantage of Central Asia

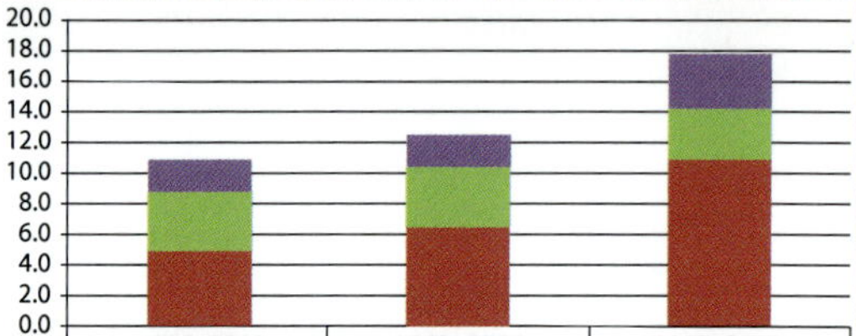

	1996–2002	2003–2007	2003–2012
Differentiated products	2.2	2.0	3.6
Reference-priced goods	3.8	3.9	3.3
Homogeneous commodities	4.9	6.5	10.9

Note: The classification follows Rauch (1999), using the 4-digit Standard International Trade Classification (SITC), Rev. 2. The classification defined homogeneous commodities as products whose price is set on organized exchanges. Products that are not traded on organized exchanges, but have a benchmark price, are defined as reference priced. Goods whose price is not set on organized exchanges and which lack a reference price are classified as differentiated.
Source: Authors' calculations based on UN Comtrade Statistics.

---

2 The revealed comparative advantage provides a useful summary for Central Asia in its transition over the past two decades. As the comparative advantage could evolve over time, a time-varying measure of revealed comparative advantage can be estimated by

$$RCA_{it}^j = \frac{exports_{it}^j}{\sum_i exports_{it}^j} \bigg/ \frac{\sum_j exports_{it}^j}{\sum_{j,i} exports_{it}^j}$$

where j denotes product, i country, and t time period.

2.3 Trade in Energy, Primary Commodities, and Manufactures

Scale and Scope of Products

Central Asia is land-rich but has low capital intensity (Figure 2.5). There are also a number of barriers that constrain trade that need to be addressed. Trade policies and regional institutions play important roles in the transition period for Central Asia, so it is essential to examine the interaction between the scale and scope of product space with capital intensity, market access, foreign investment, and institutional quality in the five Central Asian countries. There is some estimation-based evidence that infrastructure quality and endowment differences are positively associated with the size of bilateral trade of Central Asian countries with other countries (Table A3.1). Gains from trade for Central Asia will depend on how the region can expand the scale and scope of its production, and overcome a product

Figure 2.5 Endowment Triangle

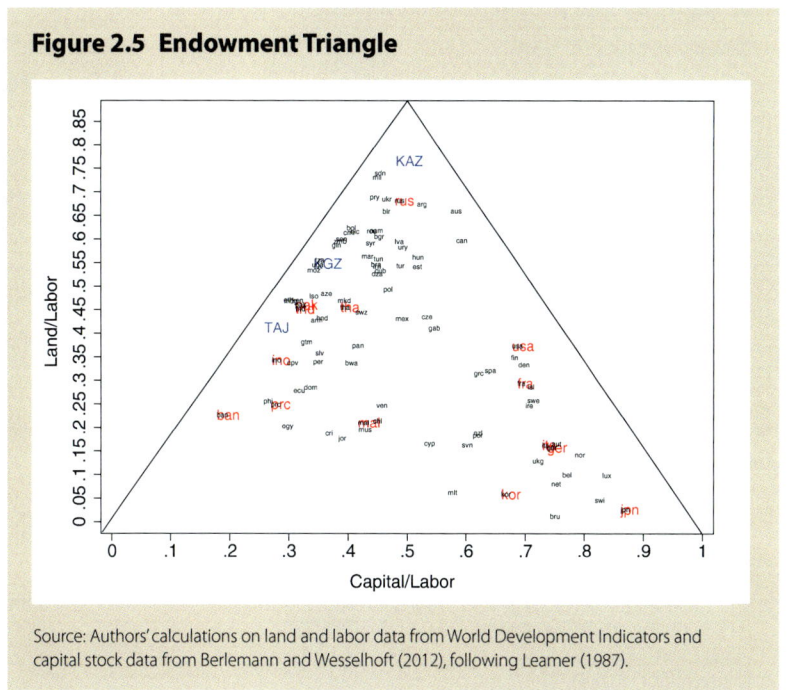

Source: Authors' calculations on land and labor data from World Development Indicators and capital stock data from Berlemann and Wesselhoft (2012), following Leamer (1987).

concentration that is based on its factor endowment (land, labor, and capital) by using new production technologies and supportive domestic institutions and regional cooperation.

Concentration of Export Products

An expansion into new varieties of products and sectors for trade may be influenced by several factors. Given the fixed costs and increasing return to scale in production, countries may want to focus on sectors that exploit their resource endowment and for which there is sufficient domestic and foreign demand, subject to transportation costs and trade facilitation. The lack of trade growth in some areas may be driven by the slow growth of demand for such products, the lack of growth of trading partners, and an unwillingness to compete in new sectors and product markets (Leamer and Stern 2009, 168–71). In the case of Central Asia, diversification of exports has always been a challenge for transition economies, as they tend to join global markets by specializing in a few goods based on their comparative advantage, mostly related to natural resources and labor-intensive products. Eventually, the transition countries will want to diversify their exports and move up the production ladder (Fujita, Krugman, and Venables 1999, 239–81). For Central Asia, there is a trade-off between the costs and benefits of export diversification. While specializing in a few products can be efficient and lead to economies of scale, excessive export concentration can divert resources and lead to overinvestment in certain industries, thereby generating diversification risks due to excessive concentration of output, production, and export revenues on only a few product categories (see Box 2.3 for garment exports from the Kyrgyz Republic).

Applying an export concentration index clearly suggests that export revenues of Central Asia are concentrated on exports of crude materials and mineral fuels, and that this concentration has grown in the past two decades (Figure 2.6).[3]

---

3   In order to examine how concentrated the exports of Central Asia are, the Herfindahl-
     Hirschman export concentration index is calculated as

$$HH_t^j = \sqrt{\sum_i \left(\frac{exports_{it}^j}{total\ exports_t^j} \right)^2}$$

where j denotes country; i product; and t time period, using UN Comtrade statistics data 4-digit SITC Revision 2.

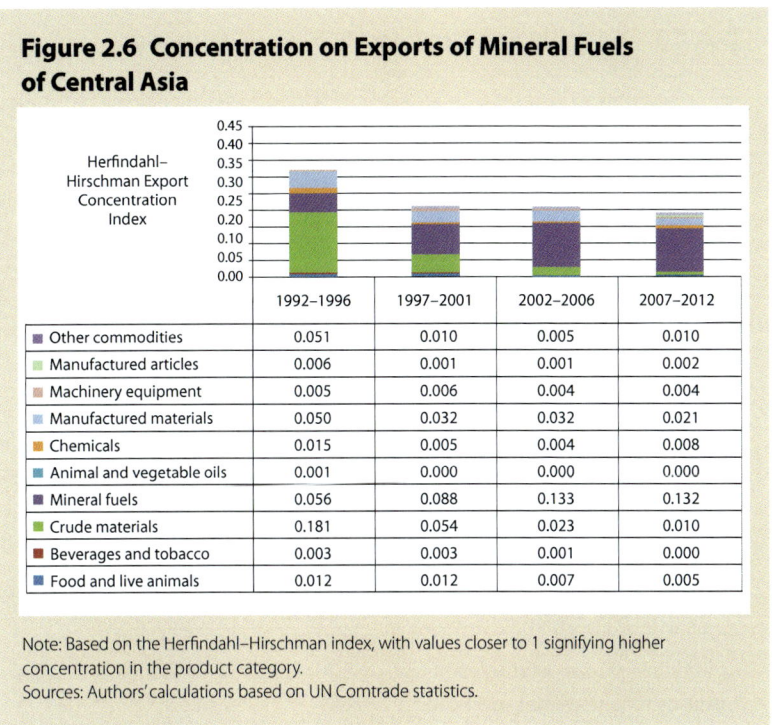

Figure 2.6 Concentration on Exports of Mineral Fuels of Central Asia

	1992–1996	1997–2001	2002–2006	2007–2012
■ Other commodities	0.051	0.010	0.005	0.010
■ Manufactured articles	0.006	0.001	0.001	0.002
■ Machinery equipment	0.005	0.006	0.004	0.004
■ Manufactured materials	0.050	0.032	0.032	0.021
■ Chemicals	0.015	0.005	0.004	0.008
■ Animal and vegetable oils	0.001	0.000	0.000	0.000
■ Mineral fuels	0.056	0.088	0.133	0.132
■ Crude materials	0.181	0.054	0.023	0.010
■ Beverages and tobacco	0.003	0.003	0.001	0.000
■ Food and live animals	0.012	0.012	0.007	0.005

Note: Based on the Herfindahl–Hirschman index, with values closer to 1 signifying higher concentration in the product category.
Sources: Authors' calculations based on UN Comtrade statistics.

However, it needs to be noted that, while UN Comtrade data provide comprehensive information across countries and industries, there are differences between national and international sources, especially those for Tajikistan, Turkmenistan, and Uzbekistan. The main components of trade for these economies, including exports of natural gas to the Russian Federation and exports of gold to other countries, are not systematically reported in national data sources. The appendix provides some data comparisons of international and national sources for Central Asia (Tables A1.3–A1.4).

Box 2.3   Garment Exports from the Kyrgyz Republic

In the 2000s, the Kyrgyz Republic's apparel sector has grown from scratch to one of the most important sectors of the economy in terms of export revenue and employment, particularly for women.

Approximately 95% of the Kyrgyz Republic's garment production is exported. Garment exports increased from US$15 million in 2003 to US$156 million in 2012. About 80% of those exports are absorbed by the Russian Federation, and most of the rest by Kazakhstan. According to official statistics, the major exports of garments are clothes for women and girls (80% of all garment exports). Currently, Kyrgyz producers provide about 2% of the Russian garment market, a considerable achievement for such a small exporting country.[a]

The garment industry is dominated by micro, small, and medium-sized enterprises. The number of apparel workers in the Kyrgyz Republic is estimated at 150,000–300,000, or 6.4% to 12.8% of total employment. The lack of precision reflects (i) a large undocumented number of apparel companies operating in the informal economy, and (ii) informal employment arrangements even at relatively formal companies in the sector, especially with regard to additional workers hired during seasonal production peaks.

Kyrgyz garment producers are dependent on imported inputs (fabric, yarn, buttons, zippers, and other accessories) and equipment. The vast majority of fabric and equipment imports come from the People's Republic of China (PRC), with the Republic of Korea and Turkey also providing inputs.

The competitive strength of the Kyrgyz garment industry is based on:

- relatively cheap labor;
- low transportation costs for inputs from the PRC;
- low import taxes for these inputs due to a special customs clearance regime;
- a lump sum taxation system for garment producers;
- producers' understanding of the requirements and tastes of low and mid-level income groups in the Russian Federation and Kazakhstan in terms of design and quality;
- well-organized industry associations effective at the policy level; and

continued on next page

Box 2.3 *continued*

- the availability of very large open markets at Dordoi (in Bishkek, capital of the Kyrgyz Republic, close to the Kyrgyz–Kazakh border) and Karasuu (near the Kyrgyz–Uzbek border), facilitating marketing and promotion of these goods in the regional markets.

High import duties imposed by the Russian Federation and Kazakhstan on imports of PRC garments also provide the Kyrgyz enterprises with a considerable price advantage.

Nevertheless, the Kyrgyz garment sector faces challenges, including insufficient access to credit, skilled labor, and higher-end inputs. Its current specialization on low- and middle-income groups in neighboring countries does not allow for production capacities to be developed that are oriented toward more remote, but also more lucrative markets in the developed countries of Asia, Europe, and North America.

The expected accession of the Kyrgyz Republic to the customs union of Belarus, Kazakhstan, and the Russian Federation would have important implications for its apparel sector. Kyrgyz producers will get even easier access to the Russian Federation's vast market if they can meet the safety and quality standards of the customs union. Meeting these standards implies that there will be some additional costs for the enterprises and for the government, which needs to provide proper quality infrastructure to support the industry. The sector is also going to be affected in two other ways: (i) the prices of fabric, equipment, and other inputs imported from the PRC will increase following the introduction of the common customs tariff of the customs union, resulting in higher production costs (negative effect for producers), and (ii) competing apparel made in the PRC will increase in price in the Kyrgyz domestic market for the same reason (positive effect for producers). Therefore, the net effect of the Kyrgyz Republic's accession to the customs union for its apparel sector is unclear.

[a] All data in this box are from the National Statistical Committee of the Kyrgyz Republic at http://www.stat.kg (accessed 5 May 2014).

2.4   Diversification of Trading Partners and Products

Extensive Margins and Intensive Margins

To achieve sustainable development, Central Asia needs to increase its trade with economic centers outside the region in terms of both intensive margins (volume and values of trade) and extensive margins (number of trading partners and number of trading products). For Central Asian economies, exports of raw materials and energy-related products are driven by demand from the major industrial economies for the raw materials and energy-related commodities. As a result, there are relatively few export market destinations. Central Asia's number of trading partners over the past 20 years has been estimated (Figure 2.7). Essentially, Central Asia not only depends on a small set of energy-related industries, services, and low-end manufactured

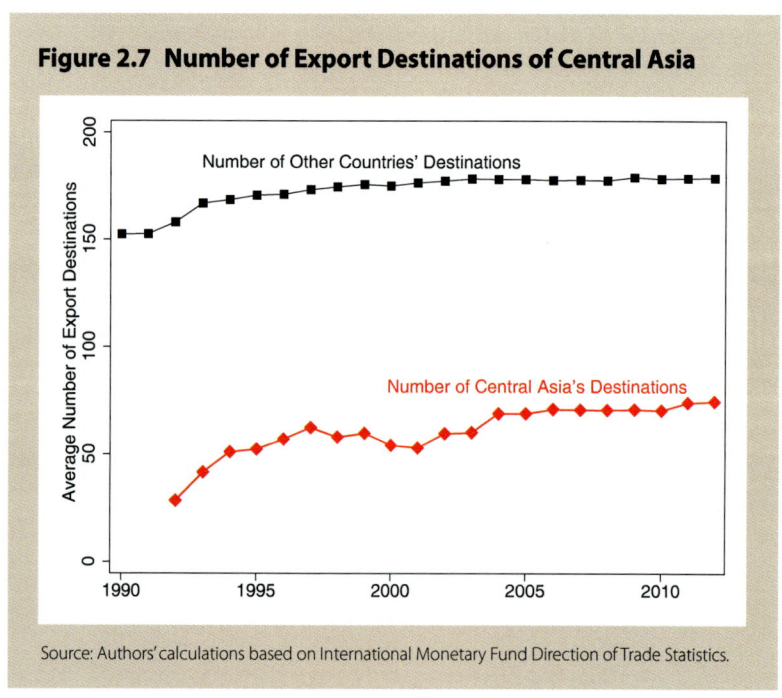

Figure 2.7 Number of Export Destinations of Central Asia

Source: Authors' calculations based on International Monetary Fund Direction of Trade Statistics.

products, it also has access to only a handful of trading partners. Both factors heighten the export risks for the region (Tables A2.1–A2.5, Figures A2.1–A2.5).

Generally, the intensity of bilateral trade relationships depends on distance, endowment differences, and similarities in the level of economic development and structure of the trading partners. For Central Asia, the transportation costs, trade facilitation, and the fixed costs of entering new markets in international trade were significant for producers and firms in these economies during their transition period. The evidence suggests that the global average number of trading-partner pairs is equal to half of all the number of country pairs existing, and this number is relatively stable over time (Helpman, Melitz, and Rubinstein 2008). For Central Asia, the existing set of trading partners is much smaller than the global average. Data estimations of Central Asia's bilateral trade suggest that differences in factor endowment influence the volume of trade with other countries (Table A3.1). Given the fixed costs and increasing returns, it remains an open issue for Central Asia to what degree it would be beneficial to increase intra-industry trade with countries with a higher level of technology and economic development. More data on consumption patterns and home-market effect (Hanson and Xiang 2004), and the conflicting forces of factor proportions and product differentiation (Romalis 2004) are needed.

More than half of all the possible country pairs between Central Asia and the rest of the world have no trade in any direction (Figure 2.8). In Helpman, Melitz, and Rubinstein (2008), it was found that about half of 158 countries have zero trade with Central Asia. Central Asia has not been able to reverse this trend in the past two decades. The evidence from Figure 2.8 suggests that Central Asia's remoteness affects its trade ties with other regions and that Central Asian countries have a much smaller number of trading partners than other countries, and this gap has persisted over the years. There is also a shortfall in the extensive margins of international trade in terms of the trading products of Central Asia. The concentration on commodities trade is smaller in the Kyrgyz Republic and Uzbekistan than in Kazakhstan, Tajikistan, and Turkmenistan (Table 2.4).

Figure 2.8 Distribution of Trading Partners Based on Direction of Trade (%)

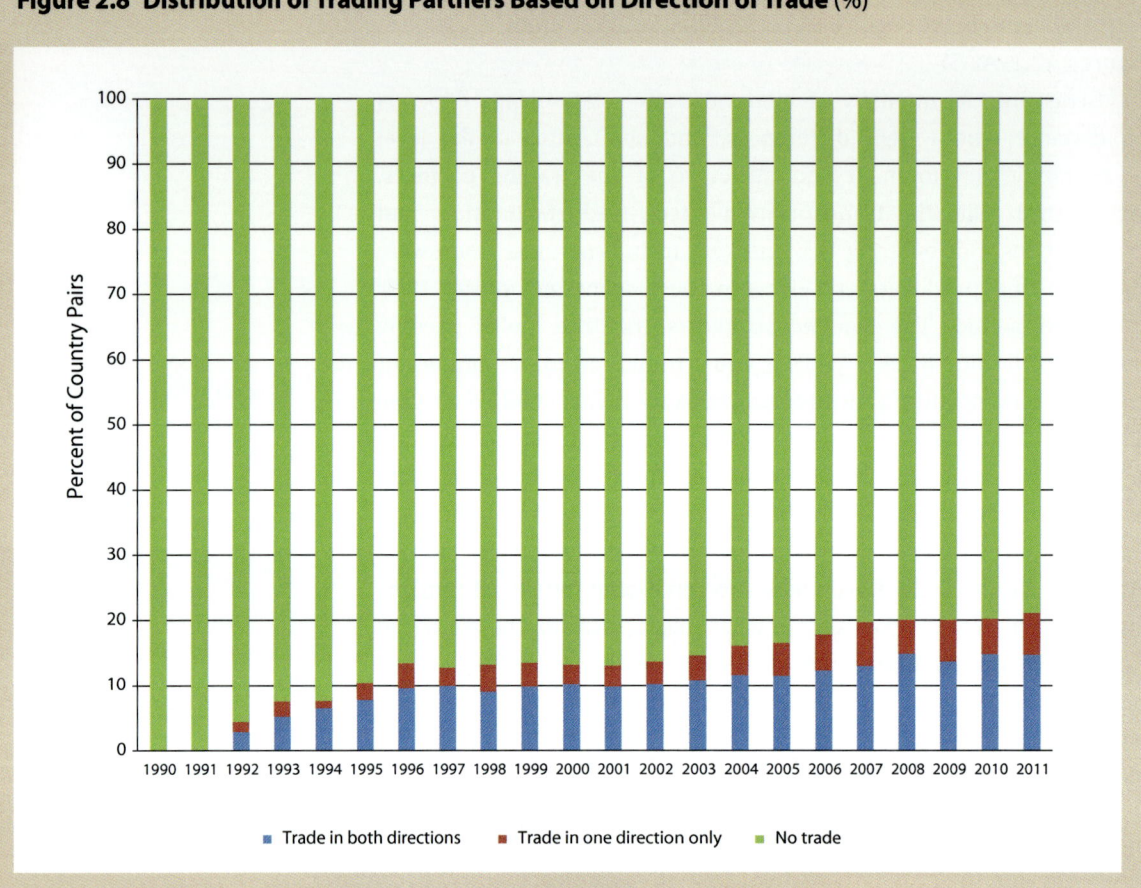

Note: This figure depicts trade relationships as a percentage of possible trading partners globally. The top part is the proportion of country pairs that do not trade (less than US$1 million) with countries in the region. The middle part is the proportion of trading partners that trade in one direction only. The bottom part represents trading partners that trade in both directions.

Source: Authors' calculations based on International Monetary Fund Direction of Trade Statistics.

Table 2.4 Product Diversification of Central Asia

Exports

Country	1996			2006			2012		
	Number of Products	Concentration Index	Diversification Index	Number of Products	Concentration Index	Diversification Index	Number of Products	Concentration Index	Diversification Index
Kazakhstan	218	0.23	0.73	199	0.60	0.75	230	0.59	0.73
Kyrgyz Republic	159	0.16	0.70	160	0.16	0.69	207	0.15	0.64
Tajikistan	100	0.42	0.78	92	0.68	0.87	131	0.51	0.79
Turkmenistan	80	0.55	0.79	92	0.70	0.80	120	0.58	0.81
Uzbekistan	170	0.53	0.78	144	0.27	0.76	174	0.23	0.65

Imports

Country	1996			2006			2012		
	Number of Products	Concentration Index	Diversification Index	Number of Products	Concentration Index	Diversification Index	Number of Products	Concentration Index	Diversification Index
Kazakhstan	246	0.07	0.44	248	0.07	0.36	251	0.07	0.35
Kyrgyz Republic	171	0.16	0.56	213	0.21	0.51	233	0.19	0.48
Tajikistan	173	0.15	0.61	210	0.15	0.52	230	0.09	0.56
Turkmenistan	205	0.10	0.53	228	0.09	0.43	238	0.09	0.46
Uzbekistan	233	0.08	0.45	224	0.10	0.42	234	0.09	0.47

Note: The concentration index is based on the Herfindahl–Hirschman index, with values closer to 1 signifying higher concentration. The diversification index estimates the differences between structure of trading products of the country and the world average; values closer to 1 suggest a larger difference from the world average.

Sources: Based on United Nations Conference on Trade and Development Statistics on Concentration and Diversification Indices of Merchandise Exports and Imports.

2.5   Gains and Costs

Gains from Trade and Distributional Conflicts

A better understanding of the gains from trade should help policy makers guide resources so they are used efficiently and productively.

Improvements in the terms of trade can serve as one indicator of whether countries gain from international trade. Measured by the ratio of export prices to import prices, the terms of trade of selected countries in Central Asia suggest that there are gains from an increase in export prices relative to import prices, thereby improving purchasing power in international markets (Figure 2.9). For Kazakhstan and Uzbekistan, there is clear evidence that the terms of trade have generally improved steadily from the late 1990s to present. However, terms of trade are volatile, which is consistent with Central Asia's concentration of export products and fluctuations of commodity prices in global markets.

Figure 2.9 Terms of Trade for Selected Central Asian Countries

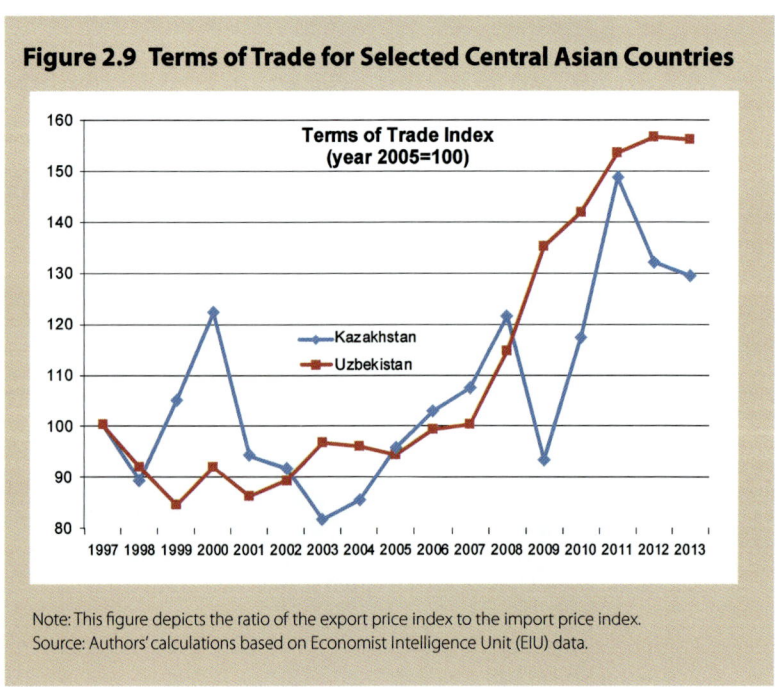

Note: This figure depicts the ratio of the export price index to the import price index.
Source: Authors' calculations based on Economist Intelligence Unit (EIU) data.

Table 2.5 Correlation between Trade Openness and Volatility of Employment and Output

Country	Correlation of Employment Volatility and Trade Openness		
	Agriculture	Industry	Services
Kazakhstan	−0.32	0.91	−0.10
Kyrgyz Republic	−0.20	0.12	−0.56
Tajikistan	−0.33	−0.06	0.29
Turkmenistan	..	..	..
Uzbekistan	−0.07	−0.50	−0.07

Country	Correlation of Output Volatility and Trade Openness		
	Agriculture	Industry	Services
Kazakhstan	−0.63	0.09	0.33
Kyrgyz Republic	−0.50	−0.60	0.14
Tajikistan	−0.46	−0.33	0.06
Turkmenistan	−0.70	−0.62	−0.60
Uzbekistan	0.71	0.46	0.53

Note: Volatility is calculated from a 3-year rolling standard deviation from 2005 to 2012. Trade openness is total trade (exports plus imports) to gross domestic product.
Source: Authors' calculations based on ADB (2013c).

An assessment of the gains and costs of extending trade ties for Central Asia needs to recognize the distributional conflicts that may result from trade openness. These include differences in returns to skilled and unskilled workers, development in rural and urban areas, the status of labor market, prospects for employment, and job creation. Data from Central Asia suggest that the relationship between trade openness and employment and output volatility is mostly negative; as countries become more open, the volatility of employment and the volatility of output declines across sectors (Table 2.5).

Nevertheless, more evidence is needed on the effects of international trade on productivity and resource reallocation, within and across sectors (Bernard, Redding, and Schott 2007).

To achieve meaningful and sustainable trade ties between Central Asia and economic centers, policy makers and regional cooperation mechanisms need to address how to compensate those who may lose from international trade in the transition period, taking into account the volatility of export earnings, the persistence of unemployment, and returns across factors of production in the region.

Other aspects of the costs and benefits of trade integration and diversification deserve further study. The intra-regional and inter-regional effects of free trade agreements and the nascent customs union between Belarus, Kazakhstan, and the Russian Federation require general equilibrium analysis, which will involve a number of assumptions. It would be useful to understand, for instance, the positive and adverse effects of the customs union on the agricultural, services, and manufacturing sectors of the member countries, on the Central Asian economies in general, and on non-member countries. In addition, strategic policy considerations are likely to play an important role in the development of various industries. Agriculture and food programs, for example, are crucial to both economic and social sustainability. The development of the automobile sector may also be promising in the context of Central Asian economies' participation in the global value chains.

2.6 Conclusions

Factor endowment, geography, infrastructure, trade facilitation, and government policies will all be important to Central Asia as it fosters trade ties with economic centers and other regions. The differences between oil exporters and non-oil exporters, and their dependence on different export commodities imply that a one-size-fits-all approach may not be suitable for the transition economies of Central Asia. Reliance on favorable world commodity prices and concentration only on a few export products may prove difficult in the future, given that natural resources will eventually be exhausted and that global commodity prices remain volatile. For its sustainable development, Central Asia needs to consider diversifying into new products and markets. A comprehensive policy agenda should attempt to overcome the sunk costs and entry barriers to new markets for Central Asian firms and producers, while taking into account the interdependence between exporting sectors and the domestic economy, as well as gains and costs in terms of output and employment as a result of greater trade openness. Skilled workers and factors associated with exporting sectors may have more to gain than unskilled workers and factors associated with sectors that compete with imports. As this possible distributional conflict applies not only to Central Asia but also its trading partners, policy makers aiming to connect Central Asia with economic centers should take into consideration gainers and losers from increased trade links.

To what extent is diversification of trade necessary for Central Asia? On the one hand, greater product differentiation, both horizontally (number of products) and vertically (quality of products), would help Central Asia to increase trade ties with major economic centers at a higher level of economic development and to expand market destinations. On the other hand, Central Asia also needs to increase production and exports in the area of its comparative advantage, taking into account the fixed costs and increasing returns in core sectors, such as oil, gas, and mineral extraction, as well as manufacturing sectors that require high capital intensity and entry barriers.

3. Foreign Direct Investment Links

3.1 Introduction

This chapter will analyze foreign direct investment (FDI) to and from countries of Central Asia. FDI is a major link between the global economy and economies of the region.

Section 3.2 covers trends in and patterns of FDI in the countries of Central Asia, including their general dynamics and structure by sector and country of FDI origin and destination. Section 3.3 provides an analysis of the impact of FDI on the economies of Central Asian republics. Section 3.4 contains a summary of findings.

3.2 Patterns of Foreign Direct Investment

Measurement of Foreign Direct Investment

During the past 10-15 years, all countries of the region have experienced strong or very strong real appreciation of their currencies against the US dollar (Figure 3.1). As a result, the purchasing power of the US dollar has fallen considerably in these economies, e.g., based on World Development Indicators data, in Kazakhstan US$1 in 2012 was equivalent to just US$0.29 in 2000. Hence, expressing the growth of FDI in current US dollars may not necessarily mean real FDI growth. Expressing FDI flows in constant 2005 US dollars gives a more accurate picture over time.

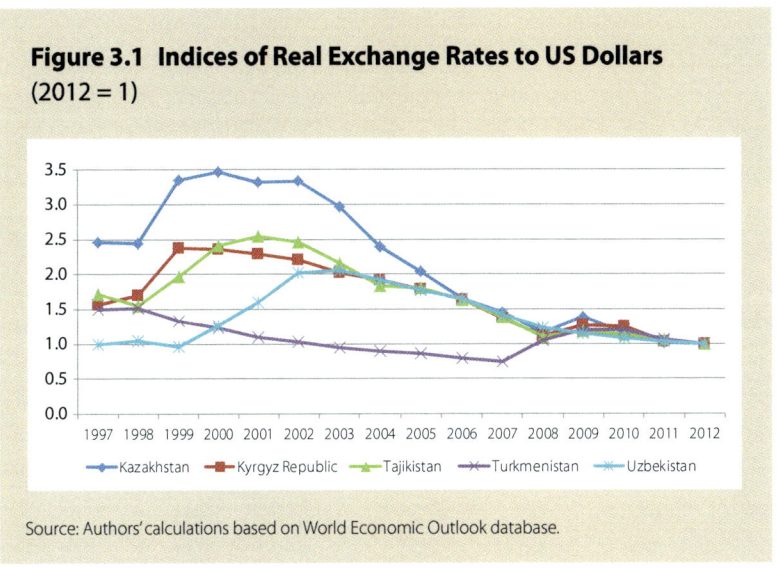

Figure 3.1 Indices of Real Exchange Rates to US Dollars
(2012 = 1)

Source: Authors' calculations based on World Economic Outlook database.

General Trends

Amounts of FDI flowing into the countries of the region vary significantly (Table 3.1). In absolute terms, Kazakhstan is the largest FDI recipient in Central Asia. In 2011, it entered the ranks of the top 20 economies of the world receiving FDI (UNCTAD 2013). Tajikistan receives the least amount of FDI; in 2010, the net inflow of FDI to this country was even negative. In relation to GDP, the largest FDI recipient in recent years (2006–2012) was Turkmenistan (Figure 3.2). Average annual FDI net inflows to this country were just below 12% of GDP, high by international standards (by this measure, Turkmenistan is ranked 26 in the world and 6 in Asia). During this period, Kazakhstan's FDI inflows exceeded 9% of GDP per annum. Uzbekistan had the lowest ratio, 2.7% of GDP.

Table 3.1 shows recent FDI flows. In the Kyrgyz Republic, Turkmenistan, and Uzbekistan, FDI inflows grew steadily over 2006–2012, while in Kazakhstan and Tajikistan they declined,[4] mainly because of the completion of several very large investment projects, which were not replaced by any comparable projects.

---

4   In Kazakhstan, a decline can be observed if the inflow is measured at constant prices or as a percentage of GDP. In current US dollars, the trend seems to be generally positive, although the 2012 nominal value is less than the 2008 level.

Table 3.1 Net Inflows of Foreign Direct Investment to Central Asia

Country	2005	2006	2007	2008	2009	2010	2011	2012
US$ million (current)								
Kazakhstan	2,546	7,611	11,973	16,819	14,276	7,456	14,287	15,117
Kyrgyz Republic	43	182	208	377	189	438	694	372
Tajikistan	54	339	360	376	16	-16	67	198
Turkmenistan	418	731	856	1,277	4,553	3,631	3,399	3,159
Uzbekistan	192	174	705	711	842	1,628	1,467	1,094
US$ million (constant 2005)								
Kazakhstan	2,546	5,942	7,864	8,966	8,913	3,890	6,364	6,575
Kyrgyz Republic	43	163	151	219	124	279	362	184
Tajikistan	54	296	259	210	9	-9	35	104
Turkmenistan	418	640	675	759	2,738	2,134	1,844	1,586
Uzbekistan	192	157	531	467	508	898	753	539
% of gross domestic product								
Kazakhstan	4.5	9.4	11.4	12.6	12.4	5.0	7.7	7.5
Kyrgyz Republic	1.7	6.4	5.5	7.3	4.0	9.1	11.2	5.7
Tajikistan	2.4	12.0	9.7	7.3	0.3	-0.3	1.0	2.8
Turkmenistan	5.2	7.1	6.8	6.6	22.5	16.1	12.1	9.4
Uzbekistan	1.3	1.0	3.2	2.5	2.6	4.2	3.2	2.1

Source: World Development Indicators.

In all five countries, FDI inflows were quite volatile; during 2006–2012, FDI inflows varied from 6.6% to 22.5% of GDP in Turkmenistan, from –0.3% to 12.0% in Tajikistan, from 5.0% to 12.6% in Kazakhstan, from 4.0% to 11.2% in the Kyrgyz Republic, and from 1.0% to 4.2% in Uzbekistan. The period under consideration includes three different phases of the global economic cycle (fast growth before the global crisis, crisis years, and post-crisis recovery), although FDI inflows in Central Asia do not seem to follow the cycle phases strictly and seem to be driven more by the time lines of large investment projects related to energy and mining.

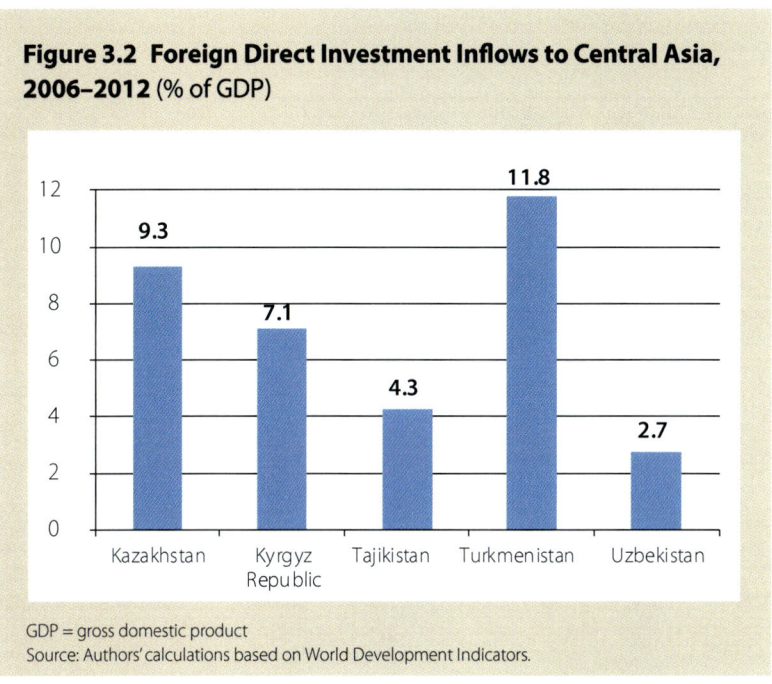

Figure 3.2 Foreign Direct Investment Inflows to Central Asia, 2006–2012 (% of GDP)

GDP = gross domestic product
Source: Authors' calculations based on World Development Indicators.

Turkmenistan and Kazakhstan have the largest FDI stocks (amount of capital, reserves, retained profits, and net indebtedness of the affiliates of FDI enterprises) (Table 3.2). However, in Kazakhstan in recent years GDP grew faster than the FDI stock, so the share of FDI stock in GDP declined by 9 percentage points between 2009 and 2012. A similar decline took place in Tajikistan for 2007–2012. This may be either just a temporary slowdown of the FDI inflow, or a result of the emergence of other GDP growth drivers (this is certainly the case for Tajikistan, where remittances are much larger than FDI). In the other three countries, the FDI stock's share in GDP shows a clear upward trend, meaning that these economies have not reached FDI saturation point yet.

Outward FDI is considerable in Kazakhstan only, which has the region's highest GDP per capita and savings. In 2007–2011, Kazakhstan's investments abroad were US$3.7 billion–US$5.0 billion (Table 3.3), but in 2012 these fell by half.

Table 3.2 Stock of Inward Foreign Direct Investment in Central Asia

Country	2005	2006	2007	2008	2009	2010	2011	2012
US$ billion								
Kazakhstan	25.6	32.9	44.6	59.0	71.8	82.6	95.4	106.9
Kyrgyz Republic	0.6	1.3	1.0	1.4	1.4	1.7	2.4	2.8
Tajikistan	0.3	0.6	1.0	0.9	1.0	1.0	1.0	1.3
Turkmenistan	2.4	3.1	4.0	5.3	9.8	13.4	16.8	20.0
Uzbekistan	1.3	1.5	2.2	2.9	3.7	5.4	6.8	7.9
% of GDP								
Kazakhstan	44.8	40.6	42.5	44.2	62.3	55.8	51.2	53.3
Kyrgyz Republic	25.5	44.3	25.9	26.8	30.5	35.4	38.9	42.6
Tajikistan	13.2	22.8	27.2	16.7	19.9	18.0	15.2	18.3
Turkmenistan	29.5	30.4	31.4	27.3	48.5	59.5	60.0	59.4
Uzbekistan	9.1	8.6	9.8	10.3	11.4	13.7	14.9	15.4

GDP = gross domestic product.
Sources: World Development Indicators, UNCTADstat.

Table 3.3 Kazakhstan's Direct Investments to Other Countries

	2005	2006	2007	2008	2009	2010	2011	2012
Flows								
US$ million (current)	429	948	4,007	3,701	4,193	3,791	5,014	2,677
US$ million (constant 2005)	429	740	2,632	1,973	2,618	1,978	2,233	1,164
% of GDP	0.8	1.2	3.8	2.8	3.6	2.6	2.7	1.3
Stocks								
US$ billion	..	..	2.2	3.3	7.1	16.2	19.9	21.0
% of GDP	..	..	2.1	2.4	6.1	11.0	10.7	10.5

.. = not available, GDP = gross domestic product.
Sources: World Development Indicators, UNCTADstat.

Foreign Direct Investment Patterns

All countries of Central Asia show similar trends of inward FDI by sector and by country of origin (Figures 3.3–3.7). By sector, there are two main streams. One is related to natural resources, including extraction of oil and gas, metals and non-metallic minerals, geological explorations; services closely related to mining, metallurgy, oil, and gas processing (including chemical industry); and, in some years, transport of energy (oil and gas pipelines). The share of these sectors in total FDI inflows in four of the countries is about or exceeds 50% of total FDI inflows (Tajikistan is the exception). The production of enterprises supported by these investments is mostly exported abroad. Projects in these sectors—development of oil and gas fields or construction of pipelines—are usually large, and their high share of the total investment portfolios of these countries results in the uneven FDI dynamics mentioned above. The start or completion of such projects leads to big changes in total FDI amounts. For example, oil and gas pipelines built by the PRC in Kazakhstan and Turkmenistan led to a hike in FDI in 2009 (the peak year of construction) and a fall in 2010, when construction was mostly completed.

Figure 3.3 Structure of Foreign Direct Investment Inflows to Kazakhstan, 2012

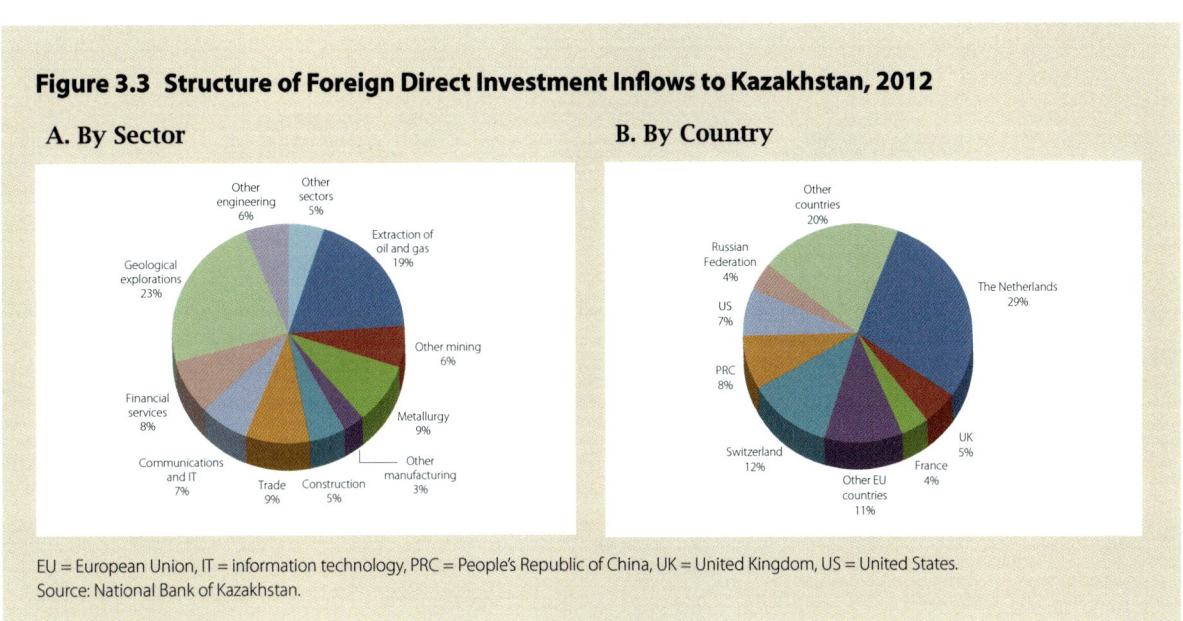

A. By Sector

Other engineering 6%
Other sectors 5%
Extraction of oil and gas 19%
Geological explorations 23%
Other mining 6%
Financial services 8%
Metallurgy 9%
Communications and IT 7%
Other manufacturing 3%
Trade 9%
Construction 5%

B. By Country

Other countries 20%
Russian Federation 4%
The Netherlands 29%
US 7%
PRC 8%
Switzerland 12%
UK 5%
France 4%
Other EU countries 11%

EU = European Union, IT = information technology, PRC = People's Republic of China, UK = United Kingdom, US = United States.
Source: National Bank of Kazakhstan.

47

Figure 3.4 Structure of Foreign Direct Investment Inflows to the Kyrgyz Republic, 2012

A. By Sector

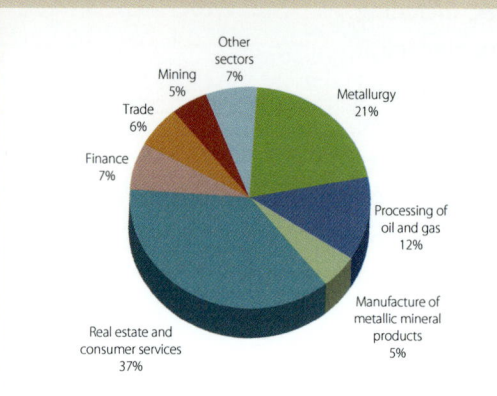

B. By Country

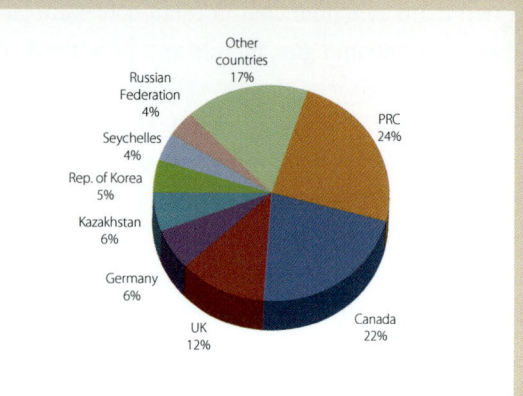

PRC = People's Republic of China, UK = United Kingdom.
Source: National Statistical Committee of the Kyrgyz Republic.

Figure 3.5 Structure of Foreign Direct Investment Inflows to Tajikistan, 2012

A. By Sector

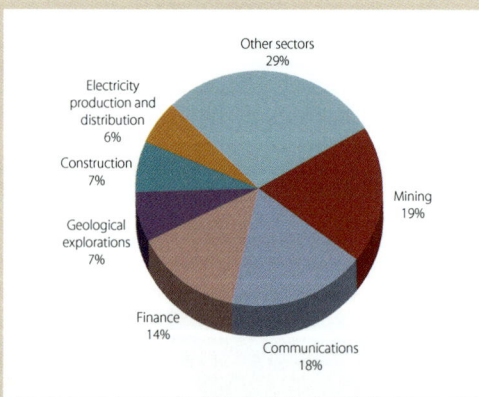

B. By Country

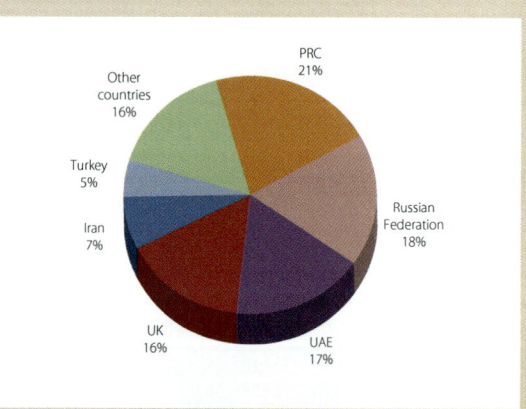

PRC = People's Republic of China, UAE = United Arab Emirates, UK = United Kingdom.
Source: Statistical Agency of the Republic of Tajikistan.

Figure 3.6 Structure of Foreign Direct Investment Inflows to Turkmenistan, 2012

A. By Sector

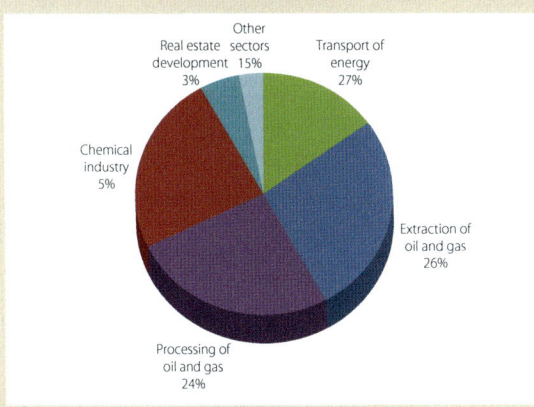

B. By Country

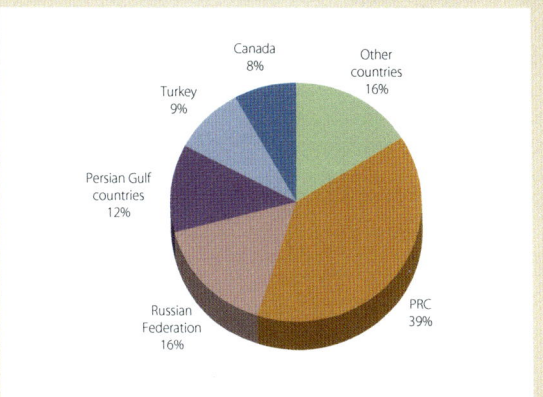

PRC = People's Republic of China.
Sources: Financial Times fDi Intelligence (2013), authors' calculations.

Figure 3.7 Structure of Foreign Direct Investment Inflows to Uzbekistan, 2012

A. By Sector

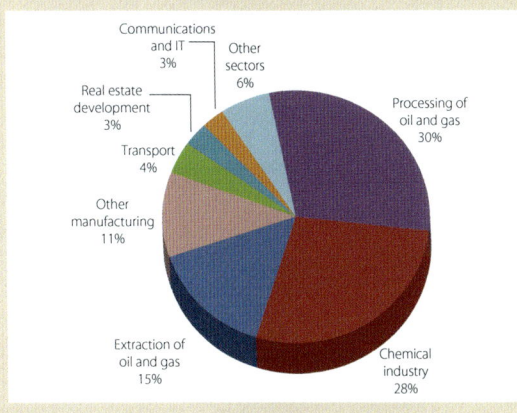

B. By Country

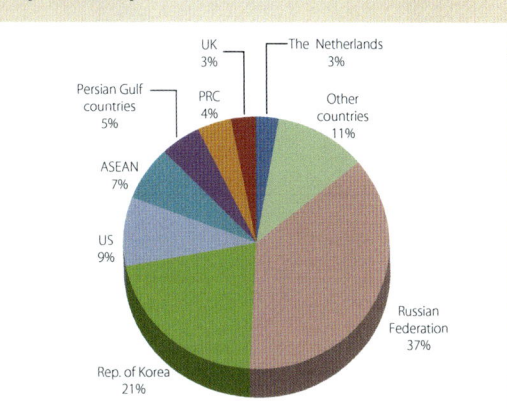

ASEAN = Association of Southeast Asian Nations, PRC = People's Republic of China, UK = United Kingdom, US = United States.
Sources: Financial Times fDi Intelligence (2013), authors' calculations.

In all Central Asia, another big stream of FDI goes to sectors serving domestic markets. These include real estate development, trade, finance, construction, and communications. The share of these sectors is especially high in the Kyrgyz Republic and Tajikistan, which do not have large hydrocarbon deposits. National data for Kazakhstan, the Kyrgyz Republic, and Tajikistan suggest that FDI into non-tradable sectors (e.g., trade, communications, real estate development, and finance) increase over time both in absolute terms and in relation to the total FDI amount. For example, in Kazakhstan, the cumulative share of trade, communications, construction, and finance in total FDI inflow increased from 8% in 2005 to 29% in 2012.[5]

Kazakhstan and Uzbekistan receive some FDI into other manufacturing industries, including machine building, food processing, and textiles. Energy and transport infrastructure receive relatively small shares of FDI, apart from hydropower plants in Tajikistan and air and railroad facilities in Uzbekistan. Public–private partnership arrangements are still at an early stage of development in the region. Agriculture receives no investments or very few investments in all these countries.

The European Union (EU), the Russian Federation, and the PRC—the main economic partners of Central Asia—are key investors to the region. However, their presence varies. The EU (mostly the Netherlands,[6] the United Kingdom, and France) is the largest source of FDI to Kazakhstan; however, in the other four countries its role is much smaller, with only the United Kingdom being a key investor.

The PRC is the main investor in Turkmenistan (39% of the total), the Kyrgyz Republic (24%), and Tajikistan (21%); its share is also significant in Kazakhstan (8%) and Uzbekistan (4%). The PRC has increased its presence in Central Asia as a direct investor over time, e.g., in 2005, the shares of the PRC in total FDI inflows to Kazakhstan and the Kyrgyz Republic were 3% and 2%, respectively; by 2012, these shares had increased to 8% and 24%. In Tajikistan, the share of the PRC in total FDI increased from 4% in 2009 to 21% in 2012.

---

5   According to data of the National Bank of Kazakhstan.

6   The Netherlands, Cyprus, and some offshore jurisdictions may not be the ultimate source of investments; often, these countries are the channels through which Russian businesses make investments in Kazakhstan (Eurasian Development Bank 2013).

The Russian Federation is one of the largest investors in all these countries; its share is the highest in Uzbekistan (37% of total FDI), quite big in Tajikistan (18%) and Turkmenistan (16%), and smaller but still visible in Kazakhstan and Kyrgyz Republic (4% in both countries).

Other big investors from outside the region, which are present in some countries of the region, include the United States, Canada, Switzerland, the Republic of Korea, Turkey, Iran, the United Arab Emirates, and other Gulf countries. Another source of investments to Central Asia is offshore jurisdictions (e.g., Cyprus, British Virgin Islands, Liberia, and Seychelles), although their role has gradually been declining over time. Investments from Singapore and some other Association of Southeast Asian Nations (ASEAN) member states as well as from Japan are present in Kazakhstan and Uzbekistan, but these countries are not key investors.

According to data from the National Bank of Kazakhstan (Figure 3.8), the sector and geographical profiles of Kazakhstan's outward investments resemble the structure of inward FDI. Key sectors (headquarter activities, extraction of oil and gas, and metallurgy) and destination countries (the Netherlands, the United Kingdom, British Virgin Islands) suggest that such outward investments are directly linked to inward FDI to Kazakhstan and may be a form of profit repatriation by foreign investors. The scale of Kazakhstan's outward investment may therefore be smaller than it appears based on nominal data.[7] Nevertheless, there are many active investment projects by Kazakh enterprises abroad, including investments by state oil company KazMunayGas in the Rompetrol Group refinery in Romania worth US$4.3 billion (Eurasian Development Bank 2013) and smaller investments to trade companies, banks, and other financial institutions in the Russian Federation, Turkey, the Kyrgyz Republic, and other countries.

---

[7] According to data from the National Bank of Kazakhstan, in 2006–2012 Kazakhstan's FDI to the Netherlands was US$23.5 billion. For the same period of time, the Financial Times fDi Intelligence database contains no investment project in the Netherlands originating from Kazakhstan.

Figure 3.8 Structure of Foreign Direct Investment Outflows from Kazakhstan, 2012

A. By Sector

B. By Country

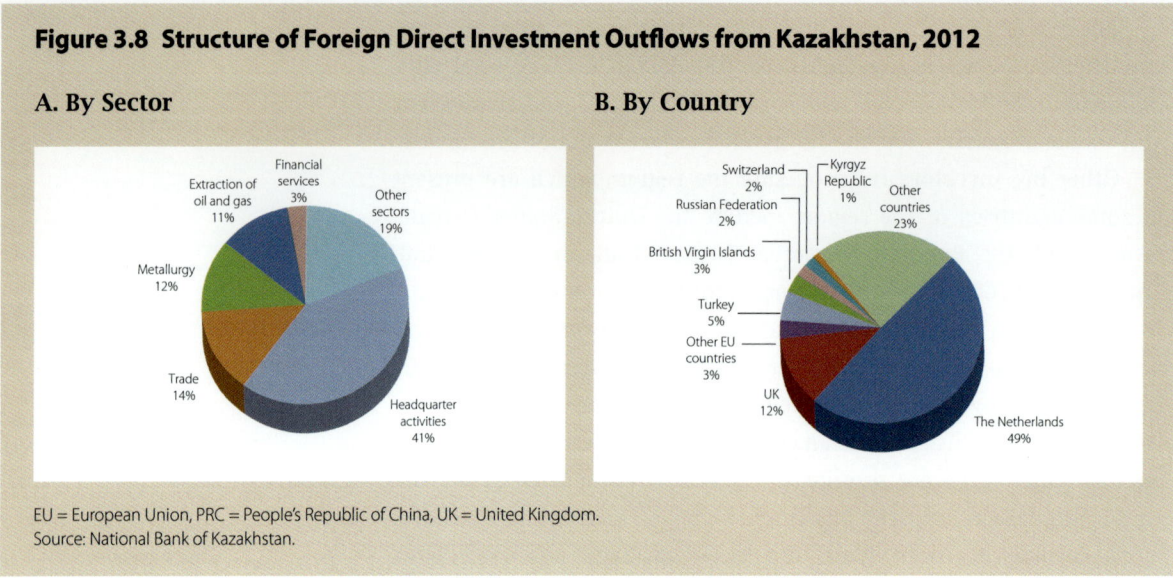

EU = European Union, PRC = People's Republic of China, UK = United Kingdom.
Source: National Bank of Kazakhstan.

3.3   Economic Impact of Foreign Direct Investment

Motives for Foreign Direct Investment

To understand the economic impact of FDI, it is useful to consider the motives driving both investors and FDI recipients when they consider investment projects. The literature on FDI identifies some typical investment motivations: resource-seeking, market-seeking, and efficiency-seeking (Dunning 1993). Resource-seeking takes place when the host country has natural resources, cheap labor, and/or physical infrastructure. Market-seeking is related to the investors' desire to expand to new markets, when it is impossible to do so through trade. This situation takes place in sectors that are either well protected from imports, or that deal with non-tradable goods and services. Efficiency-seeking FDI intends to rationalize the structure of established resource-based or market-seeking investment so the investing company can gain from the common governance of geographically dispersed activities.

In order for efficiency-seeking foreign production to take place, cross-border markets must be sufficiently open, thus this form of FDI is often a characteristic of regionally integrated markets.

For countries hosting FDI, there could be at least two different motivations. One is lack of domestic resources to develop their resource base or serve domestic markets. This motivation is usual for poor countries with low savings rates. Another motive is lack of technology, marketing links, and expertise necessary for establishing production and sales systems in investment projects.

The above discussion of FDI trends and patterns in Central Asia suggests that the key attraction for investors in all these economies is the region's natural resources: oil, gas, and metals. As noted above, projects dealing with extraction and, to a lesser extent, processing of natural resources account for more than 50% of total foreign investments into the region. In turn, the inflow of FDI into these sectors is related to the rapid growth of international commodity prices; by International Monetary Fund estimates, in 2003–2012 energy and metal prices more than tripled.

Labor does not seem to attract much investment; labor-intensive industries (e.g., textiles) are relatively minor FDI recipients, and existing investments in Turkmenistan and Uzbekistan seem to be related more to the availability of cotton rather than to the cheap labor force. An important reason for that may be that labor in the region is not cheap. The strong appreciation of regional currencies in 2000–2012 and the widespread migration of workers from Uzbekistan, Tajikistan, and the Kyrgyz Republic to the Russian Federation, Kazakhstan, and some other countries keep wages in the region relatively high, thus discouraging investments into labor-intensive sectors.

The market-seeking motive is well represented in Central Asia, as witnessed by the high share of non-tradable service sectors in the FDI portfolio (see Section 3.2). Some foreign investors into these sectors, especially in banking, may accompany their traditional partner companies or companies from their countries of origin operating in natural resource and other sectors of Central Asian economies. Also, investments in non-tradable sectors seem indirectly to depend on FDI in resource sectors because of such investments' major contribution to economic growth and, hence, the expansion of the domestic markets of the recipient countries.

Trade protectionism, which may be one of the reasons for market-seeking investments and which is practiced by some governments of the region, does not seem to attract much investment into sectors protected from inflow of imports. There is only one well-known large protection-driven investment project (the Daewoo and General Motors automobile plant in Uzbekistan), which was launched in the mid-1990s. No other manufacturing project of comparable scale unrelated to the region's natural resources has been implemented since then.

Regarding efficiency-seeking FDI, it is remarkable that, unlike in many other parts of Asia, there is little evidence of investment projects that form parts of global supply chains. One explanation for this is the notorious lack of regional cooperation, transport infrastructure, and difficulties in crossing borders. Recently, Kazakhstan established a customs union together with the Russian Federation and Belarus. The customs union started its activities in 2010 and, as a result, the customs border between Kazakhstan and the Russian Federation was eliminated. Existing evidence (ADB 2013b) indicates there has been a substantial reduction in non-tariff barriers between these two countries.[8] These developments help to create conditions for efficiency-seeking investment projects; for example, some Russian businesses may consider moving part of their activities to Kazakhstan in order to benefit from its somewhat better business environment.[9] One example of this kind of investment is the establishment of automobile production in Ust-Kamenogorsk, Kazakhstan in the form of a joint venture between AvtoVAZ (a Russian car-maker operating in partnership with Nissan and Renault) and the Kazakhstan company Asia Auto.

As for the host countries, some of them have quite substantial domestic savings (Figure 3.9), so a lack of domestic savings may be an important motive for attracting FDI only in the Kyrgyz Republic and Tajikistan. In the other three countries, a lack of technology, expertise, and marketing links seems to explain the interest of governments and local businesses in attracting competent foreign partners. As this

---

8   However, these barriers between Kazakhstan and other Central Asian countries have increased substantially.

9   According to the World Bank's Ease of Doing Business 2014, Kazakhstan is ranked 50 globally, while the Russian Federation's rank is 92. Similarly, in the Global Competitiveness Index 2012–2013, Kazakhstan and the Russian Federation are ranked 51 and 67, respectively.

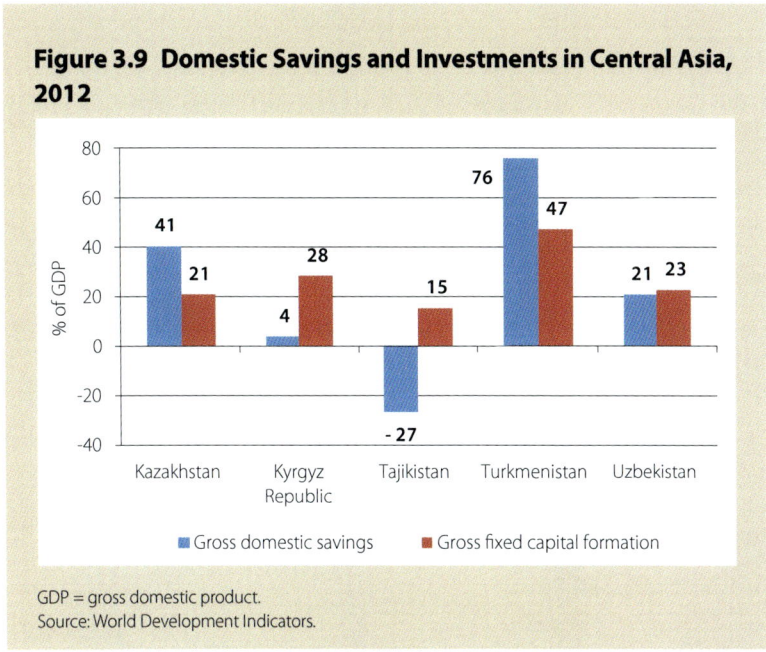

Figure 3.9 Domestic Savings and Investments in Central Asia, 2012

GDP = gross domestic product.
Source: World Development Indicators.

process of technology and skills transfer takes place, it may eventually result in a higher domestic contribution to the sectors currently relying on FDI. While Kazakhstan and Uzbekistan have articulated policies of this kind (e.g., local content requirements), there is little evidence that much learning of this type has taken place. For example, the oil and gas sector in Kazakhstan has received massive FDI and over the last decade the share of joint ventures in oil industry has increased (Figure 3.10A), implying that no catching up in purely domestic production has been observed so far. Similarly, the dependence of Uzbekistan's automobile exports on imports of vehicle parts and accessories from the Republic of Korea has not diminished over time (Figure 3.10B).

Ultimately, return on FDI is the factor driving investment decisions. Data on income from FDI are available for three Central Asian countries: Kazakhstan, the Kyrgyz Republic, and Tajikistan (Table 3.4). Since FDI income flows are volatile, figures have also been averaged for the period 2006–2012 (Figure 3.11). Returns on FDI appear to differ significantly by country. In Kazakhstan, the return rate is the highest, 25%, which is very good value for any type of investment; according to the World Development Indicators and UNCTADstat data, Kazakhstan is in the top quintile of all countries

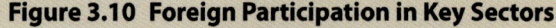

Figure 3.10 Foreign Participation in Key Sectors

A. Kazakhstan, Extraction of Oil and Gas

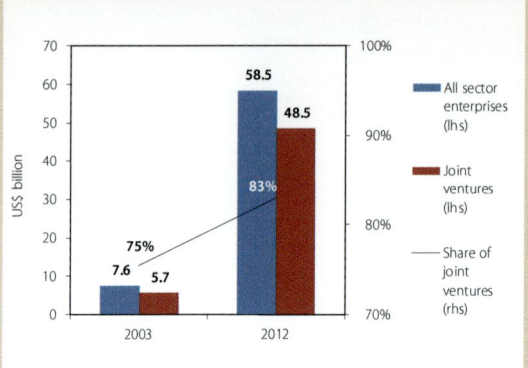

B. Uzbekistan, Automobile Production

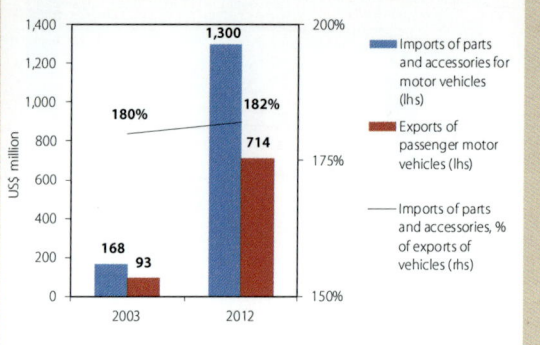

Sources: Statistical agencies of Kazakhstan and Uzbekistan.

Table 3.4 Primary Income on Foreign Direct Investment in Selected Central Asian Countries
(US$ million)

Country	2005	2006	2007	2008	2009	2010	2011	2012
Kazakhstan	4,633	7,694	11,305	16,956	10,415	17,316	24,892	24,589
Kyrgyz Republic	36	40	39	178	118	248	611	86
Tajikistan	2	46	26	4	5	9	7	33

Source: World Development Indicators.

of the world for this indicator.[10] The Kyrgyz Republic is second with a more modest, but still respectable, 12.2%. Tajikistan is last with a low rate of return of 2.1%. It is noteworthy that the countries have the same ranking on accumulated FDI stock. These return rates very much depend on the sectors receiving FDI; oil, a key recipient of FDI in Kazakhstan, is more profitable than electricity generation, which is the main recipient of FDI in Tajikistan. However, government policies allowing or disallowing investors to have high rates of return also have an impact. In the long term, one can see a clear positive correlation between the rate of return on FDI and total FDI stock.

---

10 See Sabyrova (2009) on this.

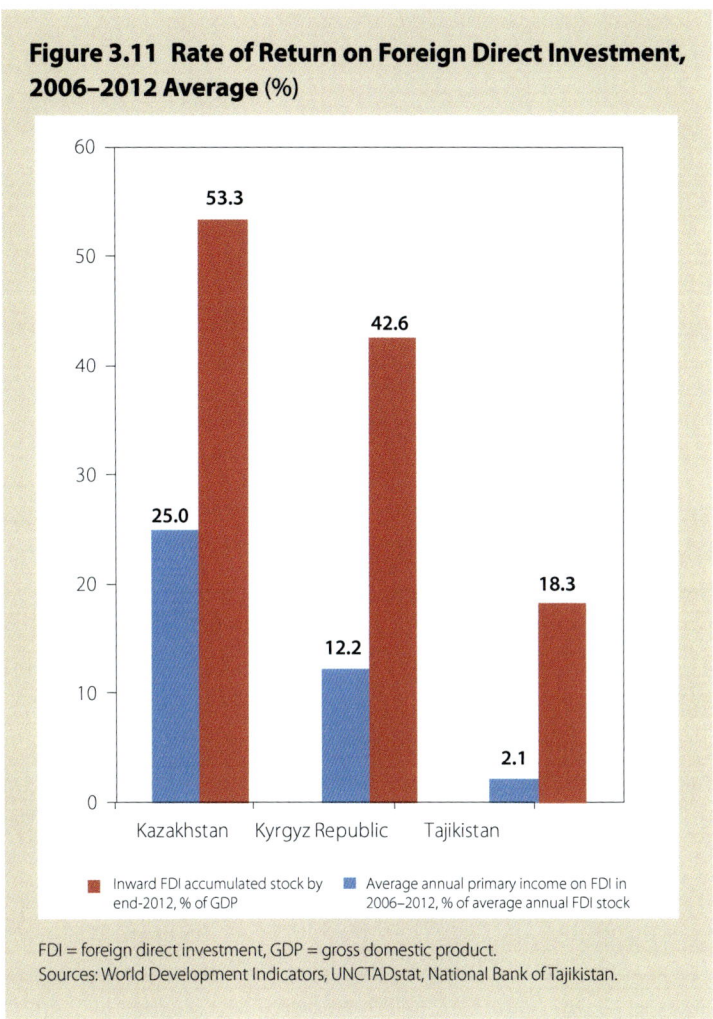

Figure 3.11 Rate of Return on Foreign Direct Investment, 2006–2012 Average (%)

FDI = foreign direct investment, GDP = gross domestic product.
Sources: World Development Indicators, UNCTADstat, National Bank of Tajikistan.

Macroeconomic Effects of Foreign Direct Investment

As discussed in Section 3.2, most Central Asian countries enjoy high rates of FDI and these influence the macroeconomic situation in all these countries. A comparison of FDI and GDP for the period of independent development of Central Asian economies (1992–2012) indicates that in all five countries FDI and GDP are correlated in the long term (Table 3.5). As expected, the strongest link (statistically

Table 3.5 Long-Term Elasticity of Gross Domestic Product with Respect to Foreign Direct Investment

Country	Elasticity	Augmented Dickey–Fuller Test for Pair Co-Integration	
		Test statistic	Test critical value (significance level)
Kazakhstan	0.25	−2.25	−1.95 (5%)
Kyrgyz Republic	0.10	−2.32	−1.96 (5%)
Tajikistan	0.13	−1.67	−1.60 (10%)
Turkmenistan	0.39	−3.59	−2.69 (1%)
Uzbekistan	0.32	−2.51	−1.96 (5%)

Sources: World Development Indicators, authors' calculations.

significant at the 1% level) is in Turkmenistan, which received the largest amount of FDI compared to the size of its economy (see Section 3.2). Here the long-term elasticity of GDP with respect to FDI is close to 0.4, i.e. a 1% increase in FDI is associated with a 0.4% increase in GDP. The weakest link between FDI and GDP is in Tajikistan, where the correlation is significant only at the 10% level. This reflects the modest and uneven FDI inflow into this country.

There are both direct and indirect transmission mechanisms from investment projects to general economic growth. Enterprises that receive FDI contribute directly to countries' gross output, exports, tax revenues, and employment. Indirectly, FDI and foreign exchange inflows caused by an increase in exports of natural resources (associated with FDI) will influence the real exchange rate and prices and wages in these economies. FDI in resource sectors may be leading to "Dutch disease" (overinvestment in commodity sectors driven by favorable commodity prices, drawing away labor from other sectors, and, as a result, rising wages and real exchange rate appreciation), signs of which have been reported in Central Asia (Egert 2013). Such indirect effects are important, but they require a separate discussion and are not considered in this report, which focuses on direct effects.

Data on operations of enterprises receiving FDI are published in Kazakhstan, the Kyrgyz Republic, and Tajikistan (Table 3.6). The contribution of these enterprises to output varies by country and is consistent with the FDI stock accumulated. In Tajikistan, enterprises

Table 3.6 Indicators of the Role of Enterprises with Foreign Participation, 2012 (% of total)

	Kazakhstan	Kyrgyz Republic	Tajikistan
Gross output	..	..	4.0
Industrial output	61.0	32.6	..
Exports	66.2	67.9	..
Employment	5.4	2.6	..

.. = not available.
Sources: Statistical agencies of Kazakhstan, the Kyrgyz Republic, and Tajikistan.

with foreign participation produce just 4% of gross output (no disaggregation by sector is available); while in Kazakhstan they produce more than 60% of total industrial output. In the Kyrgyz Republic, which is between the former two countries in terms of the FDI stock, the share of enterprises with foreign participation in total industrial output exceeds 30%. In Kazakhstan and the Kyrgyz Republic, two thirds of total exports are provided by FDI recipients.

Enterprises receiving FDI make a much smaller contribution to employment. In Kazakhstan, these enterprises' share of total employment is just 5.4% and in the Kyrgyz Republic it is 2.6%. FDI goes mostly to capital- and/or knowledge-intensive sectors (e.g., mining, geological explorations, chemical industry, communications, information technology), so the direct employment impact is small. According to the Financial Times' fDi Intelligence database, on average in Central Asian countries the creation of one new working place in these enterprises required US$543,000 in FDI. This value varies from US$586,000 per working place in Kazakhstan to US$363,000 per working place in the Kyrgyz Republic. This database lists some 700 investment projects worth US$106 billion (35% of the region's GDP in 2012), which have created employment for just 195,000 people (0.6% of the total labor force in these five countries).

Data on tax collections from enterprises receiving FDI are incomplete, but even the fragmented data available for Kazakhstan and the Kyrgyz Republic indicate that they make a major contribution to government budgets. In Kazakhstan, the main taxpayer is the oil industry, 83% of whose output is produced by joint ventures with foreign participation (Figure 3.10A). In 2012, this sector contributed an amount equivalent to US$22.9 billion (11.2% of GDP) to the National Fund of the Republic of Kazakhstan.[11] Of this amount, US$9.3 billion was transferred from the fund to the government budget and comprised 23.7% of total government revenue. In the Kyrgyz Republic, the main taxpayer is Kumtor gold mine. In 2012, Kumtor paid US$96.7 million in tax (7.1% of total tax collections or 1.5% of GDP).

3.4 Conclusions

Some countries of Central Asia (Kazakhstan, Turkmenistan) have managed to attract significant amounts of FDI; these economies are among the top investment destinations in the world. Other countries (Tajikistan, Uzbekistan) have been less successful at attracting FDI.

FDI flows in Central Asia are volatile and do not seem to follow economic cycles; their dynamics depend more on the implementation schedules of large investment projects.

Most investments are in the natural resource sectors of the Central Asian economies: extraction, processing, and transportation of hydrocarbons and metals. An important driver of these investments has been the increase in international prices for energy and other primary products. Other major and growing destinations for FDI are non-tradable service sectors, including real estate development, trade, finance, and communications. The capacity of these sectors to absorb FDI has grown rapidly in recent years in all five economies, which have benefited directly or indirectly from the resource boom in their own economies and those of their neighbors. Labor-intensive manufacturing and infrastructure received a much smaller share of FDI while agriculture received virtually nothing.

The most important investors to Central Asia are the EU, the PRC, and the Russian Federation. The PRC's investments in all economies of the region have grown very quickly. When the PRC's investments are taken together with those from the Republic of Korea, and, to a

---

11   The National Fund of the Republic of Kazakhstan is a sovereign wealth fund. Details of its activities can be found on the website of the Ministry of Finance of the Republic of Kazakhstan (http://www.minfin.gov.kz). See Kemme (2012).

lesser extent, Japan and ASEAN member states, a significant increase in the role of Asia as a source of investment resources and expertise can be seen.

FDI comes to the region in search of natural resources and new markets. The countries of Central Asia seem to be more interested in technologies and expertise provided by investors than in financial resources as some of these countries have quite substantial domestic savings.

There is a positive long-term relationship between FDI and GDP. Key transmission channels include exports by enterprises receiving FDI and taxes paid by these enterprises. The direct contribution to employment is much smaller, because FDI comes mostly to capital- rather than labor-intensive sectors.

One of the decisive factors determining the scale of FDI inflows into these economies is the rate of return on investment. There seems to be a strong positive correlation between this rate and the FDI stock accumulated in economy. In other words, in order to benefit from FDI in the long term, governments have to allow investors to benefit too.

4. Financial, Infrastructure, Institutional, and Other Links

4.1 Introduction

This chapter will study financial links, institutional ties, and other relevant connections between Central Asia and economic centers. It will continue to stress the overall themes of the study:

- transition from central planning and its net benefits, and
- shift away from orientation toward the former Soviet space.

The chapter will include financial flows, infrastructure (ports, railways, roads, and telecommunications), trade facilitation, migration and remittances, and institutional links to promote regional cooperation and international trade. People flows and knowledge transfer, which are important but difficult to quantify, are not addressed.

4.2 Patterns of Financial Flows

The financial sector is one of the most important elements of the transition to a market-based economy, and one of the most challenging. In Central Asia, financial development has been extremely uneven, both over time and across countries. Today there is a wide discrepancy between the size and composition of the five countries' financial sectors, with the most developed and varied financial sector being in

Kazakhstan, less developed financial sectors in the Kyrgyz Republic and Tajikistan, and heavy state involvement in the financial sectors of Uzbekistan and Turkmenistan.[12] Financial sector policies influence integration with neighbors because developed financial sectors can facilitate international exchange,[13] while more statist approaches permit preferential treatment of different partners.

Central Asian countries' financial sectors are not significantly integrated into global financial markets. The principal exception is Kazakhstan, whose banks began borrowing abroad as the housing bubble built up in the mid-2000s.[14] The first major foreign bank to operate as a retail bank was the Italian Unicredit, following its takeover of the ATF, a Kazakhstan bank, in November 2007. In 2007–2008, Kazakhstan suffered a major banking crisis as the housing bubble burst, and most of the country's large banks had to be bailed out in 2009 with money from the National Fund.[15] Despite the crisis, the banking sector remains more developed than elsewhere in Central Asia. Since 2010, the customs union among Belarus, Kazakhstan, and the Russian Federation appears to have stimulated mutual cross-border penetration of Russian and Kazakh banks (see Box 4.1 for the financial sector in Kazakhstan).

The post-2007 global crises affected Central Asia primarily through the sharp drops in global demand and international trade in 2008, when key commodity prices declined dramatically.

---

12 By the World Bank's headline measure, the percentage of the population aged over 15 holding an account with a formal financial institution was 42% in Kazakhstan, 23% in Uzbekistan, 4% in the Kyrgyz Republic, 3% in Tajikistan, and 0% in Turkmenistan. Data for 2011 can be found at http://datatopics.worldbank.org/financialinclusion/ (accessed 12 December 2013).

13 Less restricted capital flows can promote growth through more efficient cross-border allocation of capital, but they can also increase volatility and inhibit macro policy independence.

14 High interest rates, driven by a housing boom, attracted foreign funds in the belief that the exchange rate was fixed and bank deposits guaranteed. This was similar to earlier crises, such as in Thailand in July 1997 (Krugman 1998). The major difference was that Kazakhstan had saved about US$40 billion in the National Fund, which could be used to bail out the banks and ensure that the exchange rate did not collapse.

15 In February 2009, the state holding company Samruk-Kazyna acquired an equity stake of 75% in BTA (the country's largest credit institution) for T212.1 billion, and in May 2009 it took a 20.9% share in Halyk (the second largest bank) for T26.9 billion and a 21.2% stake in Kazkommertsbank (the third largest) for T36 billion. In January 2010, the government purchased all the shares in Alliance Bank (the fourth largest) for T129 billion, giving a 67% stake to Samruk-Kazyna and the remainder to the bank's creditors.

Box 4.1 Competitiveness of Kazakhstan's Financial Sector

Finance is one of Kazakhstan's leading economic sectors. It is dominated by banking: as of 1 January 2014, 38 institutions had banking licenses, of which 17 had foreign shareholders.

The accumulation of oil revenue in the National Fund, the growth of bank deposits as a result of economic growth, the introduction of a mandatory deposit insurance scheme, and the establishment of a fully funded pension system have all been instrumental in the growth of the financial sector. By 2007, bank lending had grown to 56% of gross domestic product (GDP), the highest level in the history of Central Asia. In the 2000s, the banking sector was the second fastest-growing sector in the economy after the oil industry. Since 2003, Kazakh banks have expanded their activities to the Russian Federation, the Kyrgyz Republic, Uzbekistan, Ukraine, Georgia, Tajikistan, and Mongolia, among others, buying local banks or opening representative offices. At the same time, the banking sector in Kazakhstan has received massive investments from the Russian Federation (Sberbank, VTB and Alfa Bank), Italy (UniCredit), the Republic of Korea (Kookmin Bank), Turkey (Bankpozitif Kredi ve Kalkinma Bankasi, part of Israeli Bank Hapoalim group), the People's Republic of China (Bank of China and Industrial Commercial Bank of China), India (Punjab National Bank), and the United Arab Emirates (investment company Alnair Capital).

With the exception of the mining sector, before the global financial crisis, private sector development in Kazakhstan was strongly dependent on the banks whose easy access to inexpensive borrowing in international capital markets enabled them to increase lending by more than 50 times over the period from 1999 to 2008 (according to the National Bank of Kazakhstan).[a] Relatively low interest rates and overly optimistic assessments of the lending portfolio quality resulted in massive lending to real estate and services companies, which led to distortions in the structure of the economy. This helped fuel a real estate bubble in 2004–2008. Risky lending practices were a major contributing factor to the economic downturn in 2008–2009 and to difficulties in the banking sector. In 2012, bank lending to the economy fell to 33% of GDP. The high level of non-performing loans (33% according to the National Bank of Kazakhstan) remains one of the main challenges for the country's banks.

The accession of Kazakhstan to the customs union with Belarus and the Russian Federation (from 1 January 2015 to become the Eurasian Economic Union) and its expected accession to the World Trade

continued on next page

Box 4.1 *continued*

Organization make the issue of the regional and global competitiveness of the country's financial sector even more important. The Global Competitiveness Index (GCI) highlighted the competitive strengths and weaknesses of Kazakhstan's financial sector (World Economic Forum 2013). Kazakhstan is ranked 50 out of 148 countries in the GCI 2013–2014, but on the competitiveness indicator its "Financial market development" is ranked only 103. The financial sector's main challenges relate to the soundness of banks, financing through local equity, and legal rights. Nevertheless, Kazakhstan outperforms other members of the customs union: Belarus is not assessed by the World Economic Forum (WEF) and the Russian Federation's financial sector is ranked only 121 (Figure B4.1.1).

Figure B4.1.1   Financial Market Development in Kazakhstan and the Russian Federation according to the Global Competitiveness Index, 2013–2014

Source: World Economic Forum (2013).

The Regional Financial Centre of Almaty, which the government hopes will become a driver of the financial sector in Kazakhstan, is ranked 58 among 83 global financial centers and 13 among Asian financial centers by the Global Financial Centers Index 15 (Z/Yen Group 2014). However, some large Kazakh companies—e.g. JSC KazMunaiGaz Exploration and Production (oil and gas), Kazakhmys PLC (copper), ENRC PLC (ferrous metals and other mining), JSC Halyk Savings Bank Kazakhstan, and JSC Kazkommertsbank—made their initial public offerings on the London Stock Exchange and not on the Almaty exchange.

[a] See http://www.nationalbank.kz/ (accessed 5 May 2014).

For Uzbekistan's two main exports, the price of cotton fell from US$0.80 per pound in March to US$0.55 in November 2008 and the price of gold fell from US$968 an ounce to US$760 over the same period. The price of oil slumped from US$149 per barrel in July to US$78 in December 2008. Although natural gas was not sold on the open market, contracts needed to be adjusted to reflect lower energy prices. The price of aluminum, Tajikistan's major export, fell from US$3,070 per ton in July 2008 to US$1,340 in February 2009, and the price of other minerals also dropped, e.g. copper fell from US$8,410 per ton in July to US$3,110 in December 2008.[16] Such price volatility highlighted the exposure of the Central Asian economies, which remained heavily dependent on a handful of primary product exports, to world prices, but as prices recovered in 2009 the economies pulled out of the trough fairly quickly.

International financial flows include FDI, which was analyzed in Chapter 3. There are significant variations across Central Asia, with foreign investment primarily in resource sectors. Only Kazakhstan is a significant outward investor, including portfolio investment by the National Fund. An important recent trend in investment flows has been the growing involvement of the PRC as a constructor of infrastructure, notably oil and gas pipelines built from Turkmenistan and western Kazakhstan to Xinjiang Uygur Autonomous Region. More recently, the PRC has diversified its investment portfolio to include participation in productive enterprises, a development highlighted by President Xi Jinping's September 2013 tour of the region.

A second major development has been the increasing importance of remittances. They have been a feature of the Tajik economy since the civil war of the 1990s, but in the 2000s remittances have become increasingly important for Tajikistan, and also for the Kyrgyz Republic and Uzbekistan. Most migrants are working in the Russian Federation, and to a lesser extent Kazakhstan, especially in the Kazakh regions contiguous to Uzbekistan (South Kazakhstan) and the Kyrgyz Republic (Almaty). The level and consequences of remittances will be analyzed in Section 4.6.

The relative magnitudes of international financial flows differ substantially across the five countries (Table 4.1), although patterns

---

16 Price data from http://www.indexmundi.com (accessed 12 December 2013).

Table 4.1 Major International Financial Flows, 2012 (US$ billion)

Country	Foreign Direct Investment	Remittances	Official Development Assistance
Kazakhstan	15.117	0.171	0.130
Kyrgyz Republic	0.372	2.308	0.473
Tajikistan	0.198	3.362	0.394
Turkmenistan	3.159	n.a.	0.038
Uzbekistan	1.094	n.a.	0.255

n.a. = not available in the source.
Notes: Remittance earnings are believed to be substantial for Uzbekistan, although less than for Tajikistan or the Kyrgyz Republic.
Sources: Foreign direct investment: chapter 3; remittances: World Bank at www.worldbank.org/migration (accessed 13 January 2014); official development assistance: Organisation for Economic Co-operation and Development at http://www.oecd.org/dac/stats/idsonline.htm (accessed 13 January 2014).

are sometimes obscured by year-on-year volatility and incomplete data.[17] FDI has overwhelmingly gone to Kazakhstan (US$15.1 billion in 2012) and Turkmenistan (US$3.2 billion in 2012). In 2012, Uzbekistan received just over US$1 billion, the Kyrgyz Republic US$0.4 billion, and Tajikistan US$0.2 billion (see Chapter 3). Remittance inflows have become very important to Tajikistan (US$3.4 billion in 2012) and the Kyrgyz Republic (US$2.3 billion in 2012); for both countries, remittance earnings exceed export revenues. For Kazakhstan, remittances have become a major outflow (US$3.8 billion in 2012) as the booming economy imported labor from other Central Asian countries. Official development assistance is tiny compared to these flows. Trade financing is also of limited importance, because primary product exports are sold under long-term contracts or on spot markets, while

---

17 Portfolio capital flows into Kazakhstan were large in 2006–2007, although the full amount owed by Kazakhstan's banks to foreign creditors is unclear. According to the *Financial Times*, in October 2007 Kazakh banks' international borrowings totaled US$40 billion, but more conservative estimates put the banks' foreign debt due in 2008 at around US$12 billion. These flows rapidly turned negative when foreign investors became aware of the asset bubble. Loans at commercial and subsidized rates have flowed from the Russian Federation and the PRC, although reports are typically of promised rather than actual flows. In 2013, China National Petroleum Company bought an 8.33% share in Kazakhstan's Kashagan oilfield for an undisclosed amount. Capital for the construction of roads in Tajikistan and the Kyrgyz Republic and the gas pipeline from Turkmenistan was not supplied on a commercial basis, although these projects clearly have economic value. In his September 2013 visit to Central Asia, PRC President Xi Jinping promised over US$50 billion in funding for energy and infrastructure projects.

manufactured imports largely enter on a cash basis. The largest annual inflow of trade finance, from the Asian Development Bank (ADB), to Uzbekistan since 2010 is no more than a quarter of a billion dollars (i.e., less than official development assistance).[18]

4.3 Financial Inclusion

As discussed in Chapter 2, to expand the international trade of Central Asia with the economic centers, the pressing policy challenge seems to be the identification of new products, markets, and potential trading partners. Major governmental efforts are needed to support the opening of new markets abroad, but an expansion into new products and markets also requires a reduction in the regulatory burden, better access to credit, and support for business start-ups and entrepreneurial activities from the formal sector (Abdih and Medina 2013). It is encouraging that the governments of Central Asia have recently taken more interest in attracting foreign investment into sectors other than natural resources, and in attempting to diversify their economies.

Central Asia can expand its international trade not only by increasing the productivity of existing exporting firms, but also by encouraging new firms to enter export markets. New firms may also help increase the export-product space (Barabasi et al. 2007) and therefore help to reduce export risks. In addition, governmental and regional efforts to help small and medium-sized firms overcome the sunk costs of entering markets in Central Asia, and vice versa, should be on the policy agenda. Policy efforts may include broad-based and targeted lending as well as export promotion policies to small and medium-sized enterprises.

---

18 ADB's Trade Finance Program (TFP) supports commercial banks offering trade finance, and Uzbekistan was one of the earliest participants in 2010 (Beck et al. 2013). As of December 2013, the TFP has been rolled out to 18 ADB members, including Tajikistan and Kazakhstan which joined in 2013. Uzbekistan is among the top six participants, having received support for 125 transactions involving US$839 million worth of trade (see http://www.adb.org/news/uzbekistan/adb-partners-two-uzbek-banks-trade-finance-program; accessed 14 January 2014). This figure appears to be over the period 2010–2013 and does not identify the value of trade finance coming from outside Uzbekistan.

There is great potential to increase trade of Central Asia as most producers and firms in the region only supply domestic markets (Table 4.2). More access to credit for small and medium-sized firms would help these firms to upgrade their production and increase opportunities of joining production networks (indirect and direct exports) and of overcoming the sunk cost barriers to entering foreign markets. Broad-based and targeted credit schemes for domestic firms, offering low interest rates, attainable collateral requirements, and an efficient loan application process, would help firms, particularly those that are not currently exporting.

Table 4.2 Survey of Firms on Export Shares and Access to Credit

	Kazakhstan	Kyrgyz Republic	Tajikistan	Uzbekistan
Number of firms surveyed	544	505	360	366
Proportion of output (%)				
Domestic sales	98.2	92.0	95.6	96.1
Indirect exports	0.8	2.2	0.6	1.9
Direct exports	1.0	5.7	3.6	2.0
Main reason for not applying for new loans or lines of credit (%)				
No need for a loan; establishment has sufficient capital	61.7	50.6	60.6	51.5
Application procedures for loans or line of credit are complex	4.3	11.6	5.3	16.0
Interest rates are not favorable	25.4	23.2	20.4	11.6
Collateral requirements for loans or line of credit are unattainable	2.0	7.9	6.2	6.7
Size of loan and maturity are insufficient	0.9	3.1	4.9	5.6
Did not think it would be approved	..	1.2	0.9	1.1

.. = not available.
Note: Surveys were carried out for Kazakhstan in 2009, the Kyrgyz Republic in 2009 and 2013, Tajikistan in 2008, and Uzbekistan in 2008.
Source: Authors' calculations based on Enterprise Surveys (International Finance Corporation).

4.4 Infrastructure and Transportation

In 1992, almost all physical transportation links from Central Asia went north to the Russian Federation. In the 1990s, the newly independent countries focused on "nationalizing" their transport networks, and regional connectivity was a low priority. While data limitations make inter-country comparisons of infrastructure quality difficult, evidence suggests that more needs to be done in Central Asia to increase its competitiveness in relation to other Asian economies (Table 4.3). This section will describe and analyze efforts to improve regional infrastructure and transport facilities, including oil and gas pipelines.

Table 4.3 Quality of Infrastructure in Central Asia

Country	Quality of Overall Infrastructure	Road	Railroad	Port	Air Transport	Electricity Supply
Kazakhstan	4.5	2.8	4.4	2.7*	4.1	4.8
Kyrgyz Republic	3.4	2.5	2.5	2.7*	3.1	2.7
Countries outside Central Asia						
PRC	4.3	4.5	4.7	4.5	4.5	5.7
Rep. of Korea	5.6	5.8	5.7	5.5	5.8	4.3
India	3.9	3.6	4.8	4.2	4.8	3.2
Indonesia	4.0	3.7	3.5	3.9	4.5	5.2
Thailand	4.5	4.9	2.6	4.5	5.5	5.2
Malaysia	5.5	5.4	4.8	5.4	5.8	5.8
Philippines	3.7	3.6	2.1	3.4	3.5	4.0
Viet Nam	3.4	3.1	3.0	3.7	4.0	4.0

PRC = People's Republic of China
Notes:
1 = worst possible situation; 7 = best situation
* Both Kazakhstan and the Kyrgyz Republic are landlocked. Quality of Infrastructure is one of the indicators used to measure global competitiveness in an annual survey conducted by the World Economic Forum. The scores are based on opinions of business leaders in a survey conducted in 148 economies.
Source: World Economic Forum (2013).

Creating National Networks

In the Soviet economy, republic borders had little significance for transport links. The newly independent Central Asian countries found that links between domestic population centers often crossed international boundaries, e.g., the Tashkent–Samarkand road passed through Kazakhstan and the Osh–Jalalabad road went through Uzbekistan, while trains from the city of Karki in Turkmenistan only went to Uzbekistan. Governments sought to avoid these new international routes by building roads to bypass the foreign section, and they prioritized national links, such as the upgraded roads from Osh to Bishkek, Ashgabat to Dashkoguz, and Dushanbe to Khujand. These steps to consolidate national transport links inevitably distracted from international links.

Over two decades later, such domestic privileging is apparent in the air networks. These provide better connections between the cities of Kazakhstan or Uzbekistan than between the national capitals of Central Asia, let alone between secondary cities in other countries (as has become common in Europe). Regional cooperation in overland transportation would benefit landlocked Central Asian countries, which rely heavily on imports and exports transiting other countries. Information sharing could improve planning and technical capacity for providing physical infrastructure.

Regional Cooperation

Despite many paper agreements both within regional groupings and on a bilateral basis, regional cooperation on infrastructure and transportation was extremely limited in the 1990s and early 2000s (ADB 2006; UNDP 2005). Even in the face of environmental disasters such as the destruction of the Aral Sea, cooperation has been elusive. Although there has been minimal implementation of practical regional cooperation among the five Central Asian countries, multilateral agencies have tried to keep the idea alive, primarily through the Central Asia Regional Economic Cooperation (CAREC) program, which brings together ADB, the European Bank for Reconstruction and Development (EBRD), the International Monetary Fund, the Islamic Development Bank, the United Nations Development Programme (UNDP), and the World Bank, and through the Special Programme for the Economies of Central Asia (SPECA) which is coordinated by the two relevant UN regional commissions (the Economic and Social Commission for Asia and the Pacific and the Economic Commission for Europe).

The CAREC program provides a forum for meetings of senior officials and discussion of trade, transport, and trade facilitation issues. The 2007 and 2008 ministerial conferences adopted a transport and trade facilitation strategy based on an expansion of six key transport corridors, which could eventually produce "economic corridors." The strategy includes a program to monitor costs in time and money of traveling along the corridors and crossing through border posts.

The Corridor Performance Measurement and Monitoring (CPMM) monthly and annual reports provide a valuable picture of the monetary costs and border delays involved in travel along the corridors.[19] Some of the physical infrastructure is good, e.g. the Tashkent–Beyneu corridor (part of the E40 route to Berlin) which has been upgraded so that speeds of 100 kilometers per hour (km/h) are possible in parts and 60 km/h on most of it. In 2012, however, crossing the border took an average of 30 hours at the Kazakhstan border post and 14 hours at the Uzbekistan post (CAREC 2012, 24). This is typical of a general pattern of some upgrading of roads but few improvements to trade facilitation. Indeed, at many border-crossing points delays have become longer, apart from those between the Russian Federation and Kazakhstan (as described in Section 4.7. on the customs union).

The longest delays are on the corridor with the highest volume of freight, the railroad from the PRC through Kazakhstan to the Russian Federation and Germany. At the border crossing between the PRC and Kazakhstan, the average time at the PRC border was 353 hours and at the Kazakhstan border 54 hours (CAREC 2012, 21). It is difficult to allocate the time to one post rather than the other because delays entering Kazakhstan lead to a back-up on the PRC border, and there is a suspicion that 2012 data are influenced by the customs union's hard line toward goods entering from the PRC. The exception to the long delays is the Chongqing–Duisburg train which has special wagons

---

19 The methodology is based on the time–cost–distance method developed by the United Nations Economic and Social Commission for Asia and the Pacific, but instead of ad hoc individual studies, CAREC's corridor performance measurement consists of regular monitoring in conjunction with the freight forwarder associations. The 2012 sample consisted of 3,194 trips, of which 80% were by road, 17% by rail, and 3% inter-modal.

to facilitate the gauge change and which is subject to simplified border formalities. Apparently, trade facilitation is possible when it has high-level support, but such support appears to be reserved for exceptional cases.

Pipelines

The most high-profile infrastructure projects have been pipelines. During the 1990s, a small gas pipeline was built from Turkmenistan to Iran. However, with low energy prices, there has been little enthusiasm among foreign investors for expensive pipeline projects, and Central Asian exporters remained dependent on the Russian monopoly Transneft. As world energy prices started to increase, the situation changed dramatically. The first private pipeline linked Kazakhstan's Tengiz oilfield to the Black Sea in 2001. In 2005, the Baku–Tbilisi–Ceyhan (BTC) pipeline provided a non-Russian outlet for Kazakhstan's oil, which could be shipped by boat to the Baku BTC terminal. This was associated with the upgrading of Aktau port, which is also an outlet for grain exports. Finally, the PRC began to invest in pipeline construction, linking Kazakhstan's Caspian oilfields to the Chinese pipeline network in 2009.

Diversification of gas pipelines was slower, but the pace picked up after 2006. The PRC built a pipeline from Turkmenistan through Uzbekistan and Kazakhstan to the western PRC. This is perhaps the best example of regional cooperation among three Central Asian governments, with Uzbekistan and Kazakhstan benefiting from transit fees and the option of exporting some of their own gas through the pipeline. The project was also striking in demonstrating the PRC's ability to negotiate and deliver the project by 2009, in contrast to the proposed Russian pipeline along the Caspian coast or the EU–backed Nabucco pipeline. These unrealized projects may now never happen as new developments in gas production have pushed down prices and technology has reduced the cost of transporting liquefied natural gas (LNG). This strengthens the position of gas producers with sea ports (e.g., Qatar or Australia) and reduces the attractiveness of building new pipelines from landlocked gas producers.[20]

---

20   As an example of the shift in the relative attractiveness of delivery modes, the Russian Federation plans to export its Arctic gas by sea, despite seasonal problems with ice, rather than by constructing pipelines to East Asian markets.

The Eurasian Land Bridge

In recent years, Central Asia has been increasingly seen as an area with dynamic neighbors, rather than as a disadvantaged landlocked region.[21] Changes in the global economy, notably the emergence of more complex global and regional value chains, have highlighted the region's locational advantages (three of the four BRIC countries—Brazil, the Russian Federation, India, and the PRC—are close neighbors).

The Eurasian land bridge rail link highlights the nexus of trade costs and global value chains. After some false starts in 2010 and 2011, regular services between Chongqing in the PRC and Duisburg in Germany were operating in 2013. They offer an attractive price and time option to electronics firms in the western PRC supplying EU markets (e.g., HP, Acer, and Foxconn) and to EU firms shipping parts to their operations to the PRC (e.g., Volkswagen, Audi, and BMW).[22] The PRC's "Develop the West" campaign was launched in 2010 and includes the idea that the PRC's western development can be enhanced by increased trade across land borders with western neighbors (Summers 2013). Rail routes from Chengdu and Zhengzhou to Europe are also being established.

The PRC proposal for a high-speed rail service that would link Shanghai to Berlin in 2 days via Astana is not implausible given the speed with which the PRC constructed its domestic high-speed rail network. The high-speed domestic line to Urumqi, where a large new rail terminus is being constructed, is scheduled for 2014 completion.

An issue in the coming decade is whether Central Asia will just collect transit fees from these developments, or whether better long-distance transport connections can be used to foster economic diversification. The answer will depend on the attractiveness of doing business in Central Asia and whether the reduction in trade costs as a result of better transport links will enable Central Asia to participate in global value chains (Box 4.2). It needs to be noted that, although the hard infrastructure of roads, railroads, ports, and pipelines is being

---

21 The problems caused by Central Asia's landlocked status have been analyzed by Raballand (2003), Grafe, Raiser, and Sakatsume (2008), Cadot, Carrère, and Grigoriou (2006), and Grigoriou (2007). Linn (2004) was one of the first to point out the potential benefits of Central Asia's location.

22 Böcking (2013) and Bradsher (2013) provide first-hand accounts.

upgraded, the effectiveness of this investment is undermined by lack of regional cooperation and the poor state of soft infrastructure, which is discussed next.

Box 4.2   A Regional Transport and Transit Hub in Uzbekistan

The Government of Uzbekistan began renovating Navoi airport in 2006 to increase its capacity and transform it into an international airport. A multimodal transport and logistics hub in Navoi was then established in 2008 by an agreement between Uzbekistan Airways and Korean Air. Since January 2009, this joint venture has enjoyed a number of preferences which in 2013 were extended for another 5 years until January 2019.[a]

The first charter cargo flight took place in April 2009. Currently Uzbekistan Airways and Korean Air are operating several cargo carriers in and out of Navoi, including the Airbus A300-600F, Boeing 777F, and Boeing 747-400F. The airport can now service three fully loaded air carriers (in the same class as the B747-400F) simultaneously and more than 20 fully loaded air carriers daily. The total capacity of the hub is 100,000 tons annually. The Navoi hub is currently linked with 21 international destinations, including major airports and logistics centers in Incheon, Milan, Brussels, Istanbul, Dubai, New Delhi, and Tianjin.

Figure B4.2.1   Cargo Transported via Navoi Hub

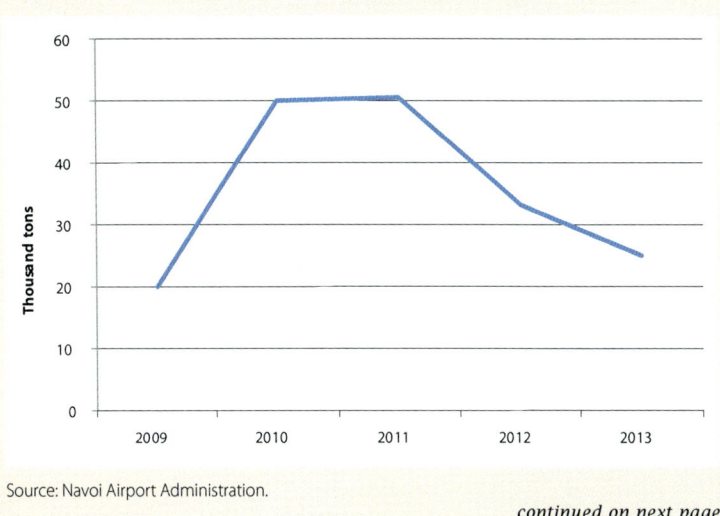

Source: Navoi Airport Administration.

continued on next page

75

Box 4.2 *continued*

The amount of cargo transported via Navoi grew steadily from 19,900 tons in 2009 to more than 50,000 tons in 2011.[b] However, in 2012 this dropped to 33,300 tons and again in 2013 to 25,000 tons.[c] The Navoi hub administration believes this is a temporary decrease related to the global economic recession—the global airfreight market shrank in 2011–2013 (IATA 2014)—and expect recovery and further growth in coming years. Plans to increase the capacity of Navoi hub from the current 100,000 to 300,000 tons were announced at the end of 2013 when Uzbekistan Airways and Korean Air extended their agreement regarding development of the international airport in Navoi for another 5 years. The Navoi hub has several advantages:

- The hub is located at the crossroads of numerous air routes in both East–West and North–South directions. This means that making a connection in Navoi could lead to a reduction in transportation costs for some freight carriers. For example, the route from Southeast Asia to Europe via Navoi is 1,000 kilometers shorter than via Dubai, resulting in a saving of about 1.5 hours and up to 15 tons of fuel (for a Boeing 747).
- Navoi airport is adjacent to the E-40 highway, which is a part of the Central Asia Regional Economic Cooperation (CAREC) corridors[d] and one of the shortest connections between Europe and the People's Republic of China. Railway lines allow access to ports in the Persian Gulf, Black Sea, and Baltic Sea. There is also a connection to Afghanistan, Pakistan, and India through the Guzar–Baysun–Kumkurgan railroad (which began operations in 2007).
- Navoi is close to Uzbekistan's historic centers, including Bukhara, Samarkand, and Khiva, which attract international tourists from all over the world.
- There are 10 capital cities with a total population of 90 million people within a 2,000-kilometer range of Navoi.
- The annual passenger flow in Navoi international airport increased from 2,586 passengers in 2007 to 45,274 in 2010.
- The Navoi hub is also linked to the Navoi Free Industrial Economic Zone (FIEZ, established in 2008), which is one of the government's flagship initiatives. The FIEZ is designed to attract foreign investments into manufacturing industries and promoting exports. Companies registered in the zone enjoy a preferential tax and customs regime, a simplified entry and stay regime for foreigners, and a special currency regulation regime. These preferences have been in place since December 2013. Currently the FIEZ hosts about 20 enterprises, which manufacture electro-technical and telecommunications equipment, machinery and computers, and pharmaceuticals, among others.

[a] Decree of the President of Uzbekistan, No. PP-1027, 31 December 2008.
[b] See Administration of Navoi International Airport at http://www.navoi-airport.com/ru/#ru/content/corporate/facts_figures/ (accessed 14 June 2014).
[c] See http://podrobno.uz/cat/economic/uzbekistan-uvelichit-moshnosti-haba-navoi/ (accessed 28 February 2014).
[d] See http://www.adb.org/countries/subregional-programs/carec.

4.5 Behind the Borders and Trade Facilitation

A central message of reports on transport, transit, and trade in Central Asia (ADB 2006) has been the importance of both hard and soft infrastructure. Trade has been hampered in the region not only by poor roads and limited rail links, but also by long delays at border crossing points and other impediments to the movement of freight. CAREC has played a role in highlighting these joint obstacles, but border crossing times remain long.

Further evidence of the woefully high costs of international trade in Central Asia is the countries' low ranking in ease of doing business indicators. In the World Bank's Doing Business 2014 rankings, in the "Trading across Borders" category, the Central Asian countries rank among the world's worst: The Kyrgyz Republic was ranked 182, Kazakhstan 186, Tajikistan 188, and Uzbekistan 189, out of 189 countries (Turkmenistan was not ranked). In the overall "Ease of Doing Business" ranking, the four countries all ranked substantially higher (Kazakhstan 50, the Kyrgyz Republic 68, Tajikistan 143, and Uzbekistan 146), implying that there is a specific crossing borders problem (Table 4.4). Such rankings must always be treated with caution, but the rock-bottom rankings on ease of trading suggest that

Table 4.4 Ease of Doing Business in Central Asia

Country	Ease of Doing Business[a]	
	Overall	Trading across Borders
Kazakhstan	50	186
Kyrgyz Republic	68	182
Tajikistan	143	188
Turkmenistan	n.r.	n.r.
Uzbekistan	146	189

n.r. = not ranked in the source.
[a] Rankings out of 189 countries.
Source: World Bank Doing Business 2014 (http://www.doingbusiness.org/rankings).

reducing the costs of international trade has not been a priority for governments in the region.

Other popular rankings have less complete coverage of Central Asia, indicating the region's poor integration into the global economy. The World Economic Forum Global Competitiveness Report covers only Kazakhstan and the Kyrgyz Republic, which rank 50 and 121, respectively, out of 148 countries surveyed. The breakdown of the rankings indicates that the two countries have relatively good policies toward trade, but that implementation is weak, and corruption is the major obstacle in both countries.[23] A survey of 108 firms involved in manufacturing, agriculture, and transportation in Kazakhstan and Uzbekistan identified informal barriers, especially "disconnected markets" and "lack of knowledge of foreign markets," as the major obstacles limiting exports.[24]

Border-crossing delays, doing business indicators showing high behind-the-border trade costs, and underdeveloped domestic financial sectors all point to a pressing need to improve the soft infrastructure associated with international trade. External assistance can, and has, contributed to upgrading hard infrastructure. Addressing issues of excessive bureaucracy and slow customs clearance, as well as more fundamental matters of implementing laws and regulations, are all matters that have to be dealt with through both domestic governments and regional cooperation.

---

[23] The report is available at http://www.weforum.org/reports/global-competitiveness-report-2013-2014. The Central Asian countries also fare poorly in the Transparency International Corruption Perceptions Index available at http://cpi.transparency.org/cpi2013/results/: Kazakhstan 140, the Kyrgyz Republic 150, Tajikistan 154, and Turkmenistan and Uzbekistan 168, out of 176 countries covered; only Iraq, Libya, South Sudan, Sudan, Afghanistan, and the Democratic People's Republic of Korea ranked below the bottom two Central Asian countries.

[24] Reported by Roman Vakulchuk and Farrukh Irnazarov on the Asian International Economists Network, 15 January 2014, at http://aienetwork.org/blog/56/overcoming-informal-trade-barriers-in-central-asia.

4.6 Migration Flows and Remittances

Although the Russian Federation's significance as a trade partner for Central Asia declined in the 1990s and its monopoly over transport routes ended, it remains an important economic partner. In particular the flow of labor from Central Asia to the Russian Federation is substantial, and remittance flows are important balance of payment items for Tajikistan and the Kyrgyz Republic.[25] These ties are pushing the Kyrgyz Republic and Tajikistan to join the customs union, which when extended to a "Eurasian Union" in 2015 will offer freer movement of labor and better treatment of migrants within the union. With the rapid growth of Kazakhstan's economy and the widening gap between the GDP of Kazakhstan and that of other Central Asian economies, a second important migration flow is into Kazakhstan; both long-term migrants and short-term labor cross the Uzbekistan border into south Kazakhstan and the Kyrgyz border to Almaty.

World Bank migration and remittances data for 2012 show remittances in 2012 of US$3,362 million in Tajikistan and US$2,308 million in the Kyrgyz Republic (Table 4.1). The remittances to GDP ratios, 44.2% in Tajikistan and 31.3% in the Kyrgyz Republic, are the highest and second highest in the world. Remittances can support economic development both directly and indirectly. The direct benefit can come if remittances are used for productive investment, either in a small business or in the education of the migrant's children. The indirect impact comes from the development of the financial sector, as more secure methods of money transfer replace the earlier practice of sending cash via friends or couriers such as transport workers.

Migrant labor has other economic and social consequences. In the short term, remittances have provided a crucial coping mechanism for poor families, and at the national level have permitted countries that are not energy-rich to import beyond their export earnings. Birkman

---

25 According to the Statistical Office of the Kyrgyz Republic, there were 457,000 migrants from the country in 2011, of which 416,000 worked in the Russian Federation. However, the EBRD (2012, 4) claims that "expert estimates" indicate the number is over 1 million. The ILO (2010) estimates that labor migration from Tajikistan amounted to 500,000–800,000 and official figures for 2012 are 877,335, but the true number is widely believed to exceed 1 million. The World Bank's migration estimates for 2010 are: Kyrgyz Republic 621,076, Tajikistan 791,618, and Uzbekistan 1,954,460.

et al. (2012) provide some evidence of the relationship between remittance inflows and the trade deficit in the Kyrgyz Republic. In the longer term, migrants acquire skills that they may bring back to their home country, or they may remain abroad constituting a "brain drain" of dynamic members of the workforce. The social consequences may be positive if unemployed young people migrate and find work, but the long-term social effects are more likely to be negative as households are broken up and social structures distorted. Many villages in Tajikistan, for example, are populated by women and children and elderly people (Box 4.3).

Box 4.3   Labor Migration from Tajikistan

The large-scale labor migration of Tajik citizens abroad during the past 15 years was caused by a severe economic recession during a conflict period in the mid-1990s. The lack of well-paid and stable employment in their own country forced many Tajiks to migrate; in 2005 (the first year for which official migration statistics are available), the number of economic migrants was 412,100 and by 2013 it had jumped to 779,400 (Kosimova 2014). Unofficial estimates for the number of economic migrants are as high as 1 million. Most migrants left their jobs and professions in Tajikistan to find unskilled jobs in the Russian Federation's construction sector.

The impact of the remittances that are regularly transferred home by migrants is very significant; the remittances are a key driver of economic development and poverty reduction in Tajikistan.

Recent studies of labor migration from Tajikistan have addressed its links to the economic situation in the Russian Federation, particularly in the context of the 2008–2009 economic crisis, and the longer-term implications for the domestic labor market and social security of migrants and their families. Danzer and Ivaschenko (2010) found that the number of migrants from Tajikistan to the Russian Federation increased as families started to send more than one family member for to look for employment abroad. They argue that remittances decreased in 2009 by more than one third of 2008 remittances levels due to the migrants' precautionary savings measures triggered by uncertainty and risks. Marat (2009) envisaged that during the crisis the migrants would need to begin looking for new employment destinations in the Russian Federation's far east and north. Umarov (2010) urged decision-makers in Tajikistan to pay greater attention to the dynamics and effects of the decrease in remittances. He compared the negative effects of labor migration to the so-called "Dutch disease"; i.e., it is no longer necessary to work hard since it is much easier to receive remittance money.

Although it is widely accepted that remittances are beneficial for Tajikistan, e.g., Olimova (2010), detailed analysis of the channels through which remittances influence the economy is very limited. In 2009, more than half of incoming remittances were spent on consumption and for more than 60% of households remittances accounted for more than half of their incomes (ILO 2010). According to Olimova (2014), preservation of the current migration patterns could negatively impact the long-term development of the country and outweigh the short-term benefits of labor migration.

Statistics on labor markets and workforces in Central Asia need to be significantly improved for the analysis to reflect reality more accurately. Data on remittances are undermined by unofficial channels of both labor and capital in and out of the Central Asian economies. While employment in the agricultural sector remains very important, the labor registration system and the informal nature of work in this sector may result in a distorted pattern of employment reallocation in Central Asia.

4.7 Institutional Links and Regional Cooperation

Following the dissolution of the Soviet Union in 1991 and the transition from central planning, the 1990s were a decade of regional disintegration for Central Asia (ADB 2006). The first decade of the 21st century showed few concrete achievements on the policy front, although the international trade of the five Central Asian economies increased substantially, driven by rising world prices for oil and gas, minerals such as gold and copper, aluminum, and (less dramatically) cotton. The direction of trade changed markedly, especially with the rising importance of the PRC as a partner.

In the second decade of the 21st century, several major changes have brought trade back on to the regional policy agenda. The Russian Federation joined the WTO in 2012 and Tajikistan in 2013, leaving Kazakhstan and Uzbekistan as the two Central Asian countries still negotiating accession. Turkmenistan does not even have observer status at the WTO. In 2010, the Russian Federation, Belarus, and Kazakhstan began implementing a customs union, and they soon encouraged other Eurasian Economic Community (EurAsEc) members, including the Kyrgyz Republic and Tajikistan, to join, potentially deepening the arrangement into a common economic space.

The World Trade Organization

WTO membership supports openness at the national level by providing a rules-based multilateral trading system. The WTO provides a forum for trade negotiations, a dispute settlement mechanism, trade

Table 4.5 World Trade Organization Status: Central Asian Countries and Neighbors

Country	Date of Application	Date of Accession
Kazakhstan	1996	--
Kyrgyz Republic	1996	1998
Tajikistan	2001	2013
Turkmenistan	No	--
Uzbekistan	1994	--
Neighboring countries		
People's Republic of China	1986	2001
India	Charter member	Charter member
Iran	1996	--
Russian Federation	1993	2012
Ukraine	1993	2008

Source: World Trade Organization website www.wto.org/

statistics and information, and training courses for negotiation and implementation of WTO agreements. While the slow progress in decade-long WTO trade talks has led to concerns about its trade negotiating function, the other functions of the WTO are useful for Central Asian economies.

The Kyrgyz Republic joined the WTO in 1998 and Tajikistan in 2013 (Table 4.5). Despite their longstanding applications, Kazakhstan and Uzbekistan have not completed the WTO accession process, perhaps due to the perception of limited benefits combined with concerns about loss of sovereignty. Turkmenistan has still not lodged an application for WTO membership.

Openness provides a basis for sustained economic growth, although if this is unaccompanied by good institutions the impact may be limited or even negative. If a country is participating in the global economy, it is desirable for it to join the WTO in order to assure trading partners that it respects international trade law and to have access to the WTO dispute resolution mechanism if a trading partner does not abide by the law.[26] The almost universal membership (159 members and 24 applicants) and the principle of consensus provide legitimacy to the WTO.

Regional Agreements

Many trade agreements have been signed among the Central Asian countries, but their impact has been minimal (Kulipanova 2012). By 2005 when the last purely Central Asian arrangement was folded into EurAsEc, the secretariats of the three significant regional agreements were all located outside Central Asia: EurAsEc in Moscow, the Economic Cooperation Organization in Tehran, and the Shanghai Cooperation Organisation in Beijing.[27] Regional cooperation in CAREC and SPECA is coordinated by multilateral institutions.

Kazakhstan's customs union with the Russian Federation and Belarus is the most significant regional integration move since 1991. The agreement was signed in November 2009, and a common external tariff and customs code established in 2010. In July 2011, customs controls at the members' common borders were abolished. The common external tariff was weighted toward the Russian tariff. The Russian Federation was able to keep 82% of its customs tariffs unchanged, lowered 14%, and increased 4% of its tariffs. Kazakhstan was able to retain 45% of its tariffs, lowering 10% of the remainder and raising 45% (Libman and Vinokurov 2012, 49). Raising external tariffs while allowing duty-free imports from the Russian Federation was a recipe for trade diversion and trade destruction. Moreover, non-tariff barriers, such as newly designed sanitary and phytosanitary rules have made it harder for the Kyrgyz Republic to export its farm products to

---

[26] A major change in the transition from the General Agreement on Tariffs and Trade (GATT) to the WTO in 1995 was the establishment of a dispute resolution mechanism, which gives greater teeth to world trade law and helps protect nations against the abuse of economic power by large trading partners. Since 1995, over 400 disputes have been ruled upon, many involving complaints by middle-income countries (e.g., 25 by Brazil, 21 by Mexico, 19 by India, 15 by Argentina, and 15 by the Republic of Korea) and in many cases the EU or US was the defendant (and, upon losing the case, complied with the ruling that a policy or practice be changed). For the full list of complaints, see http://www.wto.org/english/tratop_e/dispu_e/dispu_status_e.htm.

[27] Pomfret (2009) and Laruelle and Peyrouse (2012) provide taxonomies and analysis of the various regional agreements involving Central Asian countries. The Shanghai Cooperation Organisation is active, but largely in non-economic areas. A dense network of trade agreements within the Commonwealth of Independent States exists, although it is difficult to assess their implementation (Idrisov and Taganov 2013, Table 1).

Kazakhstan (Djamankulov 2011) and tighter controls on the customs union's external borders will discourage informal, or currently poorly monitored, imports into Kazakhstan from the Kyrgyz Republic and the PRC (Mogilevskii 2012b).[28] From an economic perspective, such trade diversion and trade destruction is negative for Kazakhstan, which will be paying more for its imports, while having a more limited choice (Pomfret 2001).

Why then did Kazakhstan take this step? Libman and Vinokurov (2012) emphasize the reassertion of Russian economic strength as an important long-run attraction of a Russian-centered regional trade arrangement, and the financial crisis of 2008 as a short-term stimulus for a defensive partnership. Mogilevskii (2012a, 33) highlights the immediate increase in tariff revenue, by at least US$1.4 billion in 2011. Laruelle and Peyrouse (2012, 44–5) see the empirical literature as indicating potential short-run benefits for Kazakhstan, but a longer-term negative impact as foreign investment, technology, and knowledge transfer flows decline.

In 2012, the Russian Federation joined the WTO and its commitments included substantial tariff reductions (to an average tariff of 8% by 2020), elimination of some non-tariff barriers to trade, and written clarification of other non-tariff measures that affect trade.[29] All of these policies will be implemented de facto as changes in the customs union's common external commercial policy, and the customs union is likely to be less harmful to Kazakhstan. Conceptually, a customs union is a second-best arrangement, which may or may not be an improvement over the preceding situation with numerous tariffs, but which is inferior to non-discriminatory trade

---

28 Laruelle and Peyrouse (2012, 44) highlight the drastic effect of the customs union on the Kyrgyz Republic's role as a platform for re-exporting PRC goods. They report estimates that the number of Kyrgyz wholesale traders fell by 70%–80% in 2010–2011. CAREC (2012, 38–9) reports that while the average border-crossing time for trucks leaving Kazakhstan for the Russian Federation fell from 7.7 hours in 2011 to 2.9 hours in 2012, the average border-crossing time for trucks entering Kazakhstan from outside the customs union increased from 8.6 to 21.5 hours, with "waiting in queue" the biggest part.

29 The Final Report on the Russian Federation's accession contains 758 pages, excluding the specific commitments on goods and services, which are in annexes, and it includes, among other things, rules for the treatment of foreign investors, constraints on trade-distorting ("amber box" in WTO terminology) agriculture subsidies, and rules on intellectual property, public procurement and foreign trade regime transparency. Shepotylo and Tarr (2012) calculated that in 2020 after the transition period the Russian Federation's weighted average bound tariff will be 8.2% and the applied tariff 7.6%.

liberalization. The empirical evidence shows that customs unions and free trade areas have generally been harmful when they have erected a wall around a protected market, but beneficial when they have low external protection and focus on integrating an internal market by trade-facilitating measures (Pomfret 2001).

In January 2012, the creation of a "common economic space" began. Its aims include the creation of a common market in goods, services, labor, and capital; coordination of monetary, financial, and tax policies; development of unified transport, energy, and information systems; and unification of systems of state support for innovation and priority sectoral development. In July 2012, the Eurasian Economic Commission, a supranational executive body comprising deputy prime ministers, was established.

How wide and how deep will the common economic space go? The beyond-trade aspects could be especially valuable for poorer Central Asian countries, which would benefit from regularizing the status of migrant workers and from resolving such issues as migrant workers' pension rights. The Kyrgyz Republic and Tajikistan, both already members of EurAsEc, are the most likely new members of the customs union,[30] preceded by the sixth EurAsEc member, Armenia. These potential new members are all in the WTO. If Kazakhstan finalizes its own WTO accession, this could reinforce steps toward an open rather than an exclusionary regionalism.

From Landlocked to Location-Blessed

Many observers have lamented that Central Asia's landlocked status is an obstacle to economic development. However, the region has the advantage of being surrounded by dynamic economies, with three of the BRICs as close neighbors; Japan, the Republic of Korea, and ASEAN rather more distant neighbors in Asia; and Turkey and the EU to the west.

---

30 A road map for the accession of the Kyrgyz Republic into the customs union is currently being negotiated by the country's government and the Eurasian Economic Commission, the governing body of the customs union. Reconciling the Kyrgyz Republic's WTO commitments with the external tariff of the customs union is a major obstacle. According to the WTO Trade Policy Review (2013, 25), 30% of Kyrgyz duties align with those of the customs union, 21% can be realigned without violating WTO commitments, and 49% would require renegotiation of WTO terms (and potentially result in compensation to affected WTO members) before they could be aligned.

The PRC's growing trade with Central Asia has been based on complementary economies, with the PRC importing raw materials (mainly oil, gas, and minerals) from and exporting manufactured goods to Central Asia. A major route for manufactures has been through the Kyrgyz Republic, from where some largely unregulated and poorly reported imports have been re-exported to the Kyrgyz Republic's neighbors. That intermediary trade has been threatened by the tightening of the customs union's external borders, and could be further threatened if the Kyrgyz Republic's accession to the customs union was associated with a tightening of the union's border with Uzbekistan. A more positive view of the future of the PRC's relations with Central Asia follows from the internal dynamic of the PRC's growth. The PRC often plays a central role in global value chains. For such networks to flourish, trade costs, in both money and time, must be low. The PRC's manufactured exports are mainly produced in the eastern coastal provinces, but in recent years the government has pursued a "look west" policy and regions such as Sichuan Province and Chongqing Municipality are now thriving. As already noted, one consequence has been the establishment of a regular rail service between Chongqing in the PRC and Duisburg in Germany, which ships components and finished goods faster than by sea and more cheaply than by air (see earlier discussion). The opportunity in coming years is for Central Asian producers to establish niches in global value chains.

Central Asia has often seen itself as a cross-road between Europe and Asia or as the core of Eurasia. This is reflected in countries' membership of two UN regional bodies (the Economic and Social Commission for Asia and the Pacific and the Economic Commission for Europe), the hosting of both European and Asian regional meetings, and participation by Central Asian countries in European and Asian sporting events. In the economic realm, this vision was evident in the Astana "Green Bridge" initiative, adopted at the Ministerial Conference on Environment and Development in Asia and the Pacific in October 2010 and approved by the Pan European Conference "Environment for Europe" in September 2011 in Astana.

The "Green Bridge" envisages Central Asia as a bridge between
- Europe and Asia and the Pacific,
- business and environment,
- developed and developing countries,
- science and practice,
- economic growth and conservation of natural resources, and
- intellectual property rights and general accessibility.

4.8 Conclusions

The changing economic relations between Central Asia and the Russian Federation and the PRC highlight the interconnected roles of comparative advantage, trade facilitation, regional agreements, and remittances in determining the level and direction of Central Asia's trade over the last two decades and for the foreseeable future. Primary product exports will remain important, and are a strong driver of increased trade with the PRC whose economy is complementary and contiguous. Labor flows are likely to continue, especially from the Kyrgyz Republic, Tajikistan, and Uzbekistan to the richer labor-scarce economies of the Russian Federation and Kazakhstan. Foreign investment is likely to focus on energy and minerals, but world prices are volatile and hard to predict. A firmer basis for sustained economic growth would be economic diversification; improvement in the ease of trading across borders and regional cooperation in transport and transit could be important precursors to this.

As most Central Asian countries and their neighbors become WTO members, how will they participate in the global economy? Will they engage in tight regional arrangements, as the Russian Federation appears to be proposing, and will this discourage closer relations with other countries in Asia or Europe? Or will they use improved transport facilities to create dynamic economic corridors running from East Asia to Europe along which producers can flourish and perhaps integrate into global value chains?

5. Policy Implications and Conclusions

5.1 Summary

Following a deep economic decline and a painful systemic transformation during the 1990s, the five Central Asian republics enjoyed good economic growth after 2000. Kazakhstan and Turkmenistan joined the group of upper-middle-income countries, and Uzbekistan is now a lower-middle-income country. The Kyrgyz Republic and Tajikistan are still classified as low-income-countries, but have an opportunity to graduate to lower-middle income status within the next 2 or 3 years.

In all five countries, growth was driven by resource exports, with spillovers to market services and government services. The recent boom was directly related to the hike in international commodity prices, which took place in the 2000s and made production of oil, gas, and metals in Central Asia and their transportation to key export markets profitable. Exports became increasingly concentrated on a handful of products: hydrocarbons, metals, and cotton. In most of the countries, the shares of manufacturing and agriculture in GDP fell.

Extraction industries and associated services (e.g., geological exploration and pipeline transport) attracted large amounts of FDI, which led to a dramatic expansion of exports by the oil- and gas-rich countries (Kazakhstan, Turkmenistan, and, to a lesser extent, Uzbekistan). In these countries, there is a strong correlation between international commodity prices, FDI, exports, and GDP growth. Countries without large hydrocarbon deposits (Kyrgyz Republic and Tajikistan) attracted less FDI (especially Tajikistan) and demonstrated less impressive export growth. However, these countries, as well as Uzbekistan, still benefited indirectly from the oil boom through labor migration to and remittances from oil-rich neighboring countries, the Russian Federation and Kazakhstan.

All of Central Asia's major international economic flows (trade, FDI, and remittances) have a high degree of geographical concentration. The PRC, the EU, and the Russian Federation (in different combinations for different countries and flows) are the main export destinations and sources of imports, FDI, and remittances. The most notable geographical diversification since 2000 has been the rise of the PRC as a major economic partner of all Central Asian countries. Other Asian partners (Republic of Korea, Japan, Gulf countries, and ASEAN) play much smaller roles, although they are still important for some countries and types of external flows.

Massive inflows of export revenue, remittances, and FDI coupled with high inflation have resulted in substantial real appreciation of Central Asia's national currencies. This has fueled growth of real wages and contributed to poverty reduction, but it has also led to a rapid expansion of non-tradable sectors and increases in imports of goods and services. Consumer goods and foods constitute a substantial part of imports. The participation of Central Asia in global value chains is mostly limited to supplies of natural resources and labor, with few examples of more complex intermediate or final tasks being undertaken in the region.

Countries of the region have tried to improve their transport infrastructure in order to improve their links to the external world. Some coordination of these activities is taking place, especially under the umbrella of CAREC and along its transport corridors. In general, however, there is a stubborn lack of regional cooperation in Central Asia, and this impedes progress in trade facilitation. Trade costs in all the five countries are very high. Recent policy changes in the region— the accession of the Russian Federation and Tajikistan to the WTO, participation of all countries but Turkmenistan in the Commonwealth of Independent States free trade area, and the formation of the customs union of Belarus, Kazakhstan, and the Russian Federation— create both opportunities and risks for regional cooperation.

5.2 Policy Implications

The current economic development model based on exporting mineral resources produced generally positive results in the 2000s, but it is associated with high risks. Countries are vulnerable to shocks that are outside their control. International commodity prices, which have been high for a long period of time, may eventually fall, leading to a contraction of natural-resource-related exports, FDI, and remittances, with adverse consequences for output, household incomes, and government revenue. While this is well understood by the governments—and economic diversification is a central item on the policy agenda in all Central Asia—the costs and benefits of diversification should deserve further studies.

Diversification requires a transition to products that are competitive in domestic, regional, and global markets. Increased competitiveness in these markets will require "behind-the-border" reforms: improvements in governance and the business climate, investments in hard and soft infrastructure, and better education and health services. Lower inflation could also contribute to competitiveness; this calls for careful use of monetary policy, but more importantly requires implementation of structural policies aimed at increasing competition and reducing transaction costs.

Integration into the global trade system is essential for countries aspiring to become producers and exporters of more diversified products. Geographical diversification of trade is related to product diversification, as efficient producers need access to world-class inputs. Outputs must be globally competitive. With Kazakhstan's WTO accession expected in 2014 or 2015, Turkmenistan and Uzbekistan will remain the only countries in the region far away from WTO membership. It is worth noting that accession costs, which may seem high for countries currently protecting their domestic market from imports, are going to be even higher if important reforms are delayed. A gradual phaseout of some protection measures and harmonization of remaining ones with the forms and level usual for WTO members should be planned and implemented systematically.

Regional preferential trade agreements have the potential to contribute to Central Asia's economic diversification. Their usefulness is positively correlated with their capacity to facilitate trade among participants and negatively correlated with the extent of trade diversion caused by the agreement. From that perspective, the Commonwealth of Independent States free trade area is useful and fairly harmless because it reinforces the already existing regime of Central Asia's trade with traditional partners based on a set of rules consistent with the WTO.

The customs union is more controversial. Recent experience provides examples of both improved trade facilitation due to the removal of the customs border between Kazakhstan and the Russian Federation, and of trade diversion due to increases in import tariffs and stricter customs administration applied by Kazakhstan to non-members. For the Kyrgyz Republic and Tajikistan, it will be important to integrate labor migration issues into their accession road maps. If the customs union does not improve their migrants' position in the labor markets of Kazakhstan and the Russian Federation, these two countries will need to assess whether the costs of losing informal trade income may be greater than the unclear benefits of possible industrial development oriented toward markets within the customs union.

The development of new and more advanced products requires investment, both domestic and FDI. All governments have policies in place to attract FDI, but many of these policies are discretionary, meaning that in order to benefit from the different types of privileges offered by the governments, investors are required to take part in long and costly negotiations with governments. This effectively serves as a pre-selection mechanism, leaving only investors interested in the most profitable activities (development of natural resources, and, to a much lesser extent, manufacturing or agriculture) and large-scale projects. Smaller foreign investors in knowledge- or labor-intensive sectors, which are capable of bringing in new technologies, products, and markets, are thereby discouraged from access to the Central Asia.

The amount of realized FDI in a country is directly correlated with the expected rate of return on investments, which means that (i) investors must be allowed to make profits, and (ii) the probability of project failure must be reduced by the provision of a regulatory environment free of risks related to confiscation of assets, renegotiation of contracts, or nonpayment by government entities for goods and services related to the project. Currently, such risks are perceived to be too high in some Central Asian countries, and need to be reduced as part of a wider commitment to more business-friendly environments and better governance. These FDI-related issues are part of a more general problem in Central Asia: regulations that seem good on paper need to be more effectively implemented.

Public policy needs to build national competences in relevant sectors. As technology and expertise transfer is one of the most important benefits brought in by FDI, it is essential that domestic workers have the education and training to carry out such transfers, and to make FDI an attractive prospect for the foreign investor. At the same time, development must be inclusive. A transition to manufacturing or service activities providing jobs for better educated segments of the labor force should not exclude those currently employed in informal trade or semi-subsistence agriculture.

Further development of the transport infrastructure is an important prerequisite for the increased integration of Central Asia into the global economy. However, physical infrastructure alone will be insufficient. Trade costs are high and unpredictable because of the current state of logistics in the region and improvements are needed in the management of cross-border and multimodal shipments, technical and administrative compliance with existing standards and norms, and exclusion of artificial barriers aimed at extortion of side payments from freight operators.

All five Central Asian countries passed through major systemic change in the 1990s as central planning was replaced by market-based economies, albeit with differing features in each country. In the 21st century, the necessary reforms may appear less drastic but they are deeper, and it is difficult to implement rapid changes without a consensus and when there are gainers and losers. To minimize social costs, countries need to avoid abrupt policy changes (e.g., dramatically increasing import tariffs in the case of customs union accession or reducing import taxes in the case of WTO accession) and to encourage the development of labor-intensive (rather than capital-intensive) enterprises, e.g., by shifting public revenue away from payroll taxes.

In addition, financial inclusion and social safety nets need to be strengthened and in oil- and gas-exporting countries, these can be funded by oil and commodity revenue funds. Small and medium-sized firms need access to credit to upgrade their production facilities and to enable them to join production networks and overcome the sunk cost barriers to entering foreign markets. Broad-based and targeted credit schemes for domestic firms, including low interest rates, attainable collateral requirements, and an efficient loan application process, are needed, particularly for the non-exporting firms in Central Asia.

Finally, policies should be as coherent as possible. Hard and soft infrastructure must improve in tandem. Transport infrastructure projects are very expensive and can be wasted if attention is not paid to their consistency with other external economic policies; for example, building transport corridors linking Central Asia with the PRC and joining a customs union with higher tariffs on imports from this major trade partner are not complementary measures. Construction of a Eurasian land bridge and of trans-regional pipelines requires regional cooperation or expensive projects will end up as white elephants. Most fundamentally, if Central Asia wishes to participate in the global value chains that are the most dynamic segment of the 21st century global economy, the countries must simultaneously improve the ease of doing business and the predictability and cost of international transactions, especially if they are to connect with manufacturing centers in Asia (see Box 5.1 for development priorities in Central Asia).

Box 5.1 Development Policy Priorities for Oil Exporters and Non-Oil Exporters

Countries endowed with natural resources such as oil and gas tend to depend on the export receipts from these natural resources as the main source of national revenues. Because natural resources are exhaustible, countries need to ensure that the revenues derived from them are properly managed. In addition, the terms of trade of natural resources are subject to volatility in the global commodity markets, which lends some uncertainty to the economic outlook of natural resource exporters.

continued on next page

Box 5.1 *continued*

Table B5.1.1 Development Priorities of Oil Exporters and Non-Oil Exporters

Development Policies	Oil Exporters	Non-Oil Exporters
Monetary and fiscal management	Same as non-oil exporters, plus oil fund management and the utilization of foreign reserves and sovereign wealth funds	• Current account convertibility • Macro-prudential policies • Trade liberalization and WTO membership • Tax collection and fiscal management • Market-determined flexible exchange rates
Competitiveness and corporate governance	Same as non-oil exporters, plus incentives for technology transfer in the oil and gas sectors	• Investor-friendly business procedures • Laws and regulations for competition and corporate governance • Credit guarantees and support for small and medium-sized enterprises • Compensation measures for sectors affected by structural reforms • Diversification of industries and export products
Infrastructure and transportation	Same as non-oil exporters, plus oil and gas pipeline development	• Integration of regional road, rail, and air transport • Operation of telecommunications, electricity, transportation • Independent and efficient regulation • Formulation of energy strategy
Banking and capital markets	Same as non-oil exporters, plus measures to avoid financial bubbles as a result of revenue windfalls	• Deposit insurance system • Law and regulations • Private pension funds • Deepening of financial sector • Financial education and better access to credit to households and small businesses
Social reform	Same as non-oil exporters, plus environmental protection for resource extraction activities	• Expenditure on health and education • Water supply and sanitation in rural area • Poverty reduction and inequality • Social security and social safety nets
Regional cooperation and integration	Same as non-oil exporters, plus cooperation in energy security	• Customs systems and trade facilitation • Free trade agreements

Sources: Authors' compilation; Asian Development Outlook (2014); Dowling and Wignaraja (2006).

While there are overlaps in the development priorities for the Central Asia's oil- and gas-exporting economies (Kazakhstan, Turkmenistan, and Uzbekistan) and the non-oil-exporting economies (Kyrgyz Republic and Tajikistan), there are also a number of differences between the two groups. The rich endowment of natural resources can be both a blessing as well as a challenge.

Appendix 1
Statistical Data on Central Asia

This section provides a general overview of available data on the external links of Central Asian countries. It does not attempt to cover all types of economic and social data; it concentrates on trade and investment data. Some other types of data are also briefly discussed later.

Statistical standards. All five countries of the region maintain a dialogue with the International Monetary Fund (IMF) on statistical data issues. Kazakhstan and the Kyrgyz Republic subscribe to the IMF's special data dissemination standard (SDDS), which aims to produce and disseminate timely and comprehensive economic and financial data. Tajikistan participates in the IMF's general data dissemination system, which is a data quality improvement framework and is less demanding than SDDS. Turkmenistan and Uzbekistan do not participate in either the SDDS or the general data dissemination system.

Trade data.[1] A standard source of information on the merchandise trade of different countries is the United Nations Commodity Trade Statistics Database (UN Comtrade). This database contains export and import values and physical quantities disaggregated by trade partner and commodity. However, for Central Asia the database has many gaps. Only Kazakhstan and the Kyrgyz Republic have regularly reported trade data to UN Comtrade since 1995. Tajikistan reported data for 2000 only; Turkmenistan supplied data from 1997 to 2000; and Uzbekistan has never reported trade data.

UN Comtrade data on exports and imports of Kazakhstan and the Kyrgyz Republic are also incomplete. In July 2010, with the creation

---

1   This trade data discussion is adapted from Mogilevskii (2012c).

of the customs union of Belarus, Kazakhstan, and the Russian Federation, trade within the customs union was registered differently from trade with other countries. Therefore, 2010 data for Kazakhstan only partially reflect its trade with other members of the customs union. However, since 2011 the dataset for this country has become complete again. In the case of the Kyrgyz Republic, export values for some commodities are included in the totals in the reports to UN Comtrade, but they are not shown separately.

In Kazakhstan, the Kyrgyz Republic, and Tajikistan, practically all the data missing from UN Comtrade are available from websites and publications of national statistical agencies and customs agencies. Turkmenistan and Uzbekistan publish only aggregate data on their foreign trade flows. More detailed data on these countries are sometimes available in secondary sources, such as publications by local authors. Another resource is the IMF's Direction of Trade Statistics (DOTS), which provides data on bilateral trade totals for almost all possible pairs of countries, but not on the commodity structure of trade.

One source of disaggregated data, often used in the absence of official trade data, is mirror statistics provided by trade partners. This information source also does not always work in Central Asia. Some key export items, such as natural gas in the case of Turkmenistan and Uzbekistan, or gold in the case of the Kyrgyz Republic and Uzbekistan, are not reported or are reported only partially by importing countries. Additionally, some important trade partners of Central Asian countries do not report to UN Comtrade, such as Iran in 2007–2009 and 2012, and Central Asian countries themselves do not consistently report trade with each other.

Moreover, many trade data from Central Asian countries are inaccurate and biased because of weak registration systems, special import tax schemes which do not require precise reporting of import values (as in the Kyrgyz Republic), or the widespread evasion of import tax payment in all Central Asian countries. Because of this widespread tax evasion, in Central Asia (unlike in other parts of the world) export data, which in most cases are not associated directly with any tax liabilities, are more reliable than import data. Discrepancies in trade partners' data strongly suggest the existence of considerable informal cross-border trade flows.

Foreign direct investment (FDI) data. Data on FDI in Central Asian countries are fragmented. International databases—the World Bank's World Development Indicators, the IMF's Balance of Payments Statistics, and UNCTADstat—provide country-level data on total amounts of inward and outward FDI only. The Financial Times' fDi Intelligence database provides detailed data on investment projects for all five countries, but these relate to greenfield investments and start only in 2003. The Eurasian Development Bank's data on outward FDI of four Eurasian countries provide information on Kazakhstan's large investment projects. Detailed data on the geographical and sector structure of FDI are published by statistical agencies and/or central banks of Kazakhstan, the Kyrgyz Republic, and Tajikistan; these data are mostly consistent with those provided by international organizations.

Other economic and social data. In all these economies, the informal sector is very big, ranging from 20% to 50% depending on the country and estimation method. Therefore, all official gross domestic product (GDP) data need to be taken with caution and treated as minimum estimates.

The size of the informal sector also has implications for labor market statistics. Employment in sectors where informal activities are widespread (especially agriculture, retail trade and consumer services, and construction) can be estimated with only a low degree of precision. The number of labor migrants from the Kyrgyz Republic, Tajikistan, and Uzbekistan to the Russian Federation, Kazakhstan, and some other countries is unknown; estimates vary greatly, are often based on anecdotal evidence, and tend to be exaggerated. In labor-migrant-sending countries, many migrants are still counted as agricultural workers (based on their traditional occupation and permanent place of living). In migrant-receiving countries (such as Kazakhstan), informal migrant workers from neighboring countries may not be included in labor force and employment data.

Estimates of migrants' remittances are also subject to error. Estimates are based on data from the Central Bank of Russia on transborder transfers made by individuals through money transfer operators and assume that the Russian Federation is the main destination of migrants and the main source of remittances. These estimates are then somehow adjusted for transfers from countries other than the Russian Federation and via other transfer channels. The assumptions used for these calculations are often unknown and may be associated with systematic measurement errors; for example, in the Kyrgyz Republic, a large part of transfers from the Russian Federation made by individuals may not be workers' remittances, but revenue for exporters and re-exporters.

Unemployment data are more reliable in those countries that use the International Labour Organization (ILO) definition of unemployment and routinely run labor force surveys as part of their household survey (Kazakhstan and Kyrgyz Republic). The other three countries have neither accepted the ILO definition, nor generate data to which this definition could be applied. Similarly, a poverty measurement system based on a national household survey is available in Kazakhstan and the Kyrgyz Republic. Tajikistan periodically runs a living standards measurement survey, which is based on the World Bank's methodology. Uzbekistan carried out such a survey once in 2003.

Uzbekistan still has a multiple exchange rate system with a street exchange rate for US dollars that exceeds the official rate by 30%–40%. Turkmenistan had a similar system until 2009, when exchange rates were unified. In these countries, estimates of GDP and other economic variables in US dollars with a large non-tradable component calculated on the basis of official exchange rates seem likely to be overestimates.

Many caveats are needed when dealing with data in Central Asia. Nevertheless, by combining different types of data and being aware of existing sources of bias and errors, a consistent and meaningful interpretation of data, and hence an understanding of the economic and social trends and patterns in these economies, is still possible.

Table A1.1 Data Sources

Main Variables	Description	Source
Total trade	Data on bilateral trade flows are taken from the United Nations Commodity Trade Statistics Database (UN Comtrade) and the International Monetary Fund's (IMF) Direction of Trade Statistics (DOTS). Total trade is a summation of the export and import value of a product traded at the 1-digit level of SITC2 classification, for the five Central Asian countries, over the period 1992–2012. The unit of this variable is the US dollar.	UN Comtrade, IMF DOTS, Economist Intelligence Unit (EIU)
Imports	Bilateral imports into Central Asia at the 1-digit level of SITC2. The unit of this variable is the US dollar.	UN Comtrade, EIU
Exports	Bilateral exports from Central Asia at the 1-digit level of SITC2. The unit of this variable is the US dollar.	UN Comtrade, EIU
Net exports	The difference between exports and imports. As this report is concerned with the value of trade, the absolute value of net exports has been chosen. The unit of this variable is the US dollar.	UN Comtrade, EIU
Trade dependence	A ratio between net exports and the total labor force. This variable is presented as a percentage.	UN Comtrade, World Development Indicators (WDI)
Labor force	Data on the total labor force for each country are derived from WDI, which defines the total labor force in accordance with the International Labour Organization definition which includes the economically active population who can supply labor for the production of goods and services during a specified period (aged 15 and older). This includes the armed forces, the unemployed, and first time-job-seekers, but excludes workers in the informal sector. This variable is presented as number of people.	WDI
Real gross domestic product (GDP)	Extracted from Penn World Tables 8.0. Real GDP is presented in US dollars.	Penn World Tables 8.0
Distance	A bilateral distance based on geographic coordinates of the capital cities. This variable is measured in kilometers.	CEPII's GeoDist Databases
Common border	A binary variable that equals 1 if importer and exporter are neighbors with a common physical boundary and 0 otherwise.	CEPII's GeoDist Databases
Common official language	A binary variable that equals 1 if importer and exporter share a common official language and 0 otherwise.	CEPII's GeoDist Databases

continued on next page

Table A1.1 *continued*

Main Variables	Description	Source
Common language ethno-linguistic group	A binary variable that equals 1 if a language is spoken by at least 9% of the population in both countries and 0 otherwise.	CEPII's GeoDist Databases
Colony	A binary variable that equals 1 if both countries have ever had a colonial link and 0 otherwise.	CEPII's GeoDist Databases
Common colony	A binary variable that equals 1 if both countries have had a common colonizer after 1945 and 0 otherwise.	CEPII's GeoDist Databases
Business startup costs	Taken from WDI. It is measured as a percentage of gross national income (GNI) per capita.	WDI
Trade facilitation	An overall assessment of (i) ability to track and trace consignments, (ii) competence and quality of logistical services, (iii) ease of arranging competitively priced shipments, (iv) efficiency of customs clearance processes, (v) frequency with which shipments reach the consignee within scheduled or expected time, and (vi) the quality of trade and transport-related infrastructure. The performance is rated on a scale of 1 (lowest) to 5 (highest).	WDI
Revealed comparative advantage (RCA)	Ratio of the share of a country's total exports of a commodity in its total exports over the share of world exports of the same commodity in total world exports. RCA is calculated according to Rauch's classification of commodity groups. RCA can range from 0 to $+\infty$. A product is said to have a revealed comparative advantage if the value exceeds 1. Rauch (1999), using commodity segregation at 4 digits SITC Rev. 2, classified goods into three categories. The classification defined homogeneous goods as products whose price is set on organized exchanges. Products that are not traded on organized exchanges, but have a benchmark price, are defined as reference priced. Goods whose price is not set on organized exchanges and which lack a reference price are classified as differentiated.	Authors' calculation
Trade intensity	Ratios of total bilateral trade over the GDP of the trading partners.	Authors' calculation
Export concentration	The Herfindahl-Hirschman index is calculated for export concentration at 1 digit SITC Rev. 2. The Herfindahl-Hirschman index is defined as the square root of the sum of the squared shares of exports of each 1-digit level SITC in total exports for the country under study. The index ranges between 0 and 1. Higher values mean that exports are concentrated in few sectors.	Authors' calculation

SITC = Standard International Trade Classification.

Table A1.2 Product Classifications and Economy Abbreviations

Product Classifications	
0	Food and live animals
1	Beverages and tobacco
2	Crude materials, inedible, except fuels
3	Mineral fuels, lubricants, and related materials
4	Animal and vegetable oils, fats, and waxes
5	Chemicals and related products, not elsewhere specified
6	Manufactured goods classified chiefly by material
7	Machinery and transport equipment
8	Miscellaneous manufactured articles
9	Commodities and transactions not classified elsewhere

Economy Abbreviations

Afghanistan (AFG), Albania (ALB), Algeria (DZA), American Samoa (ASM), Andorra (AND), Angola (AGO), Anguilla (AIA), Antigua and Barbuda (ATG), Argentina (ARG), Armenia (ARM), Aruba (ABW), Australia (AUS), Austria (AUT), Azerbaijan (AZE), Bahamas (BHS), Bahrain (BHR), Bangladesh (BAN), Barbados (BRB), Belarus (BLR), Belgium (BEL), Belize (BLZ), Benin (BEN), Bermuda (BMU), Bhutan (BHU), Bolivia (Plurinational State of) (BOL), Bonaire, Saint Eustatius and Saba (BES), Bosnia and Herzegovina (BIH), Botswana (BWA), Brazil (BRA), British Virgin Islands (VGB), Brunei Darussalam (BRU), Bulgaria (BGR), Burkina Faso (BFA), Burundi (BDI), Cambodia (CAM), Cameroon (CMR), Canada (CAN), Cape Verde (CPV), Cayman Islands (CYM), Central African Republic (CAF), Chad (TCD), Chile (CHL), People's Republic of China (PRC), Colombia (COL), Comoros (COM), Congo (COG), Cook Islands (COO), Costa Rica (CRI), Côte d'Ivoire (CIV), Croatia (HRV), Cuba (CUB), Curaçao (CUW), Cyprus (CYP), Czech Republic (CZE), Democratic People's Republic of Korea (PRK), Democratic Republic of the Congo (COD), Denmark (DEN), Djibouti (DJI), Dominica (DMA), Dominican Republic (DOM), Ecuador (ECU), Egypt (EGY), El Salvador (SLV), Equatorial Guinea (GNQ), Eritrea (ERI), Estonia (EST), Ethiopia (ETH), Faeroe Islands (FRO), Falkland Islands (Malvinas) (FLK), Fiji (FIJ), Finland (FIN), France (FRA), French Guiana (GUF), French Polynesia (PYF), Gabon (GAB), Gambia (GMB), Georgia (GEO), Germany (GER), Ghana (GHA), Gibraltar (GIB), Greece (GRC), Greenland (GRL), Grenada (GRD), Guadeloupe (GLP), Guam (GUM), Guatemala (GTM), Guernsey (GGY), Guinea (GIN), Guinea-Bissau (GNB), Guyana (GUY), Haiti (HTI), Holy See (VAT), Honduras (HND), Hong Kong, China (HKG), Hungary (HUN), Iceland (ISL), India (IND), Indonesia (INO), Iran (Islamic Republic of) (IRN), Iraq (IRQ), Ireland (IRE), Isle of Man (IMN), Israel (ISR), Italy (ITA), Jamaica (JAM), Japan (JPN), Jersey (JEY), Jordan (JOR), Kazakhstan (KAZ), Kenya (KEN), Kiribati (KIR), Kuwait (KWT), Kyrgyz Republic (KGZ), Lao People's Democratic Republic (LAO), Latvia (LVA), Lebanon (LBN), Lesotho (LSO), Liberia (LBR), Libya (LBY), Liechtenstein (LIE), Lithuania (LTU), Luxembourg (LUX), Macao, China (MAC), Madagascar (MDG), Malawi (MWI), Malaysia (MAL), Maldives (MLD), Mali (MLI), Malta (MLT), Marshall Islands (RMI), Martinique (MTQ), Mauritania (MRT), Mauritius (MUS), Mayotte (MYT), Mexico (MEX), Micronesia (Federated States of) (FSM), Monaco (MCO), Mongolia (MON), Montenegro (MNE), Montserrat (MSR), Morocco (MAR), Mozambique (MOZ), Myanmar (MYA), Namibia (NAM), Nauru (NAU), Nepal (NEP), The Netherlands (NET), New Caledonia (NCL), New Zealand (NZL), Nicaragua (NIC), Niger (NER), Nigeria (NGA), Niue (NIU), Norfolk Island (NFK), Northern Mariana Islands (MNP), Norway (NOR), Oman (OMN), Pakistan (PAK), Palau (PAL), Panama (PAN), Papua New Guinea (PNG), Paraguay (PRY), Peru (PER), Philippines (PHI), Pitcairn (PCN), Poland (POL), Portugal (POR), Puerto Rico (PRI), Qatar (QAT), Republic of Korea (KOR), Republic of Moldova (MDA), Réunion (REU), Romania (ROU), Russian Federation (RUS), Rwanda (RWA), Saint Helena (SHN), Saint Kitts and Nevis (KNA), Saint Lucia (LCA), Saint Pierre and Miquelon (SPM), Saint Vincent and the Grenadines (VCT), Saint-Barthélemy (BLM), Saint-Martin (French part) (MAF), Samoa (SAM), San Marino (SMR), Sao Tome and Principe (STP), Saudi Arabia (SAU), Senegal (SEN), Serbia (SRB), Seychelles (SYC), Sierra Leone (SLE), Singapore (SIN), Sint Maarten (Dutch part) (SXM), Slovakia (SVK), Slovenia (SVN), Solomon Islands (SOL), Somalia (SOM), South Africa (ZAF), South Sudan (SSD), Spain (SAP), Sri Lanka (SRI), State of Palestine (PSE), Sudan (SDN), Suriname (SUR), Svalbard and Jan Mayen Islands (SJM), Swaziland (SWZ), Sweden (SWE), Switzerland (SWI), Syrian Arab Republic (SYR), Tajikistan (TAJ), Thailand (THA), The former Yugoslav Republic of Macedonia (MKD), Timor-Leste (TIM), Togo (TGO), Tokelau (TKL), Tonga (TON), Trinidad and Tobago (TTO), Tunisia (TUN), Turkey (TUR), Turkmenistan (TKM), Turks and Caicos Islands (TCA), Tuvalu (TUV), Uganda (UGA), Ukraine (UKR), United Arab Emirates (ARE), United Kingdom of Great Britain and Northern Ireland (UKG), United Republic of Tanzania (TZA), United States of America (USA), United States Virgin Islands (VIR), Uruguay (URY), Uzbekistan (UZB), Vanuatu (VAN), Venezuela (Bolivarian Republic of) (VEN), Viet Nam (VIE), Wallis and Futuna Islands (WLF), Western Sahara (ESH), Yemen (YEM), Zambia (ZMB), Zimbabwe (ZWE).

Table A1.3 Data Comparisons: International and National Sources (US$ billion)

Trade Values		World Development Indicators					National Statistics				
Year	Goods and Services	KAZ	KGZ	TAJ	TKM	UZB	KAZ	KGZ	TAJ	TKM	UZB
2000	Exports	10.35	0.57	0.85	2.77	3.38	--	--	--	--	--
	Imports	8.98	0.65	0.87	2.35	2.96	--	--	--	--	--
2001	Exports	10.17	0.56	0.73	2.88	3.20	--	--	--	--	--
	Imports	10.40	0.56	0.85	2.72	3.15	--	--	--	--	--
2002	Exports	11.58	0.64	0.80	3.08	2.99	11.6	--	0.76	--	--
	Imports	11.59	0.70	0.93	2.38	2.84	8.9	--	0.92	--	--
2003	Exports	14.93	0.74	0.98	3.72	3.78	15	0.74	0.88	--	--
	Imports	13.27	0.87	1.14	3.38	3.10	10.4	0.87	1.14	--	--
2004	Exports	22.65	0.94	1.21	4.22	4.84	18.9	0.94	--	--	--
	Imports	18.95	1.13	1.45	4.07	3.93	11.5	1.12	--	--	--
2005	Exports	30.59	0.95	0.60	5.27	5.42	19.8	0.94	--	--	--
	Imports	25.55	1.42	1.22	3.87	4.10	13.2	1.39	--	--	--
2006	Exports	41.43	1.18	0.66	7.51	6.33	--	1.07	0.25	--	--
	Imports	32.79	2.24	1.62	3.59	5.36	--	1.60	0.91	--	--
2007	Exports	51.84	2.01	0.77	9.55	8.85	--		0.62	--	--
	Imports	44.82	3.20	2.55	4.90	8.15	--		2.14	--	--
2008	Exports	76.40	2.75	0.86	12.35	12.17	--	3.03	--	--	12.15
	Imports	49.56	4.76	3.70	7.78	11.40	--	4.74	--	--	11.39
2009	Exports	48.48	2.57	0.75	15.08	11.68	48.2	2.69	--	--	11.53
	Imports	39.00	3.69	2.71	9.15	11.70	39	3.68	--	--	11.69
2010	Exports	65.14	2.47	0.99	17.23	12.45	65.7	3.90	--	--	12.45
	Imports	42.93	3.92	2.96	10.04	11.22	44.3	4.61	--	--	11.21
2011	Exports	92.88	3.38	1.13	21.84	15.00	92	--	--	--	15
	Imports	51.82	5.06	3.68	12.73	14.17	51.7	--	--	--	14.16

Sources: Authors' calculations based on national statistics drawn from International Monetary Fund Article IV Consultation Reports and international statistics from World Development Indicators.

Table A1.4 Data Discrepancies between National and Mirror Statistics

Country	4-digit HS Statistics on Imports of Light Industry Products	Reporter	2005	2010
Kazakhstan	Value of imports into Kazakhstan (US$ million)	Kazakhstan	92	145
		PRC	1,956	4,731
		Discrepancy ratio	21	33
	Weight of imports into Kazakhstan ('000 tons)	Kazakhstan	62	50
		PRC	122	391
		Discrepancy ratio	2	8
Kyrgyz Republic	Value of imports into the Kyrgyz Republic (US$ million)	Kyrgyz Republic	21	195
		PRC	563	3,130
		Discrepancy ratio	26	16
	Weight of imports into the Kyrgyz Republic ('000 tons)	Kyrgyz Republic	53	205
		PRC	57	378
		Discrepancy ratio	1	2
Tajikistan	Value of imports into Tajikistan (US$ million)	Tajikistan	..	..
		PRC	29	837
		Discrepancy ratio	..	..
	Weight of imports into Tajikistan ('000 tons)	Tajikistan	..	..
		PRC	14	10
		Discrepancy ratio	..	..

.. = not available, HS = Harmonized Commodity Description and Coding System, PRC = People's Republic of China.
Sources: Mogilevskii (2012c), based on UN Comtrade statistics and statistics agencies of Kazakhstan, the Kyrgyz Republic, and Tajikistan.

Appendix 2
Major Trading
Partners of Central
Asian Republics

Table A2.1 Kazakhstan: Trading Partners, 2012
(exported and imported goods valued at US$10 million or more)

Trading Partner	Exports (US$ million)	Trading Partner	Imports (US$ million)
People's Republic of China	16,484	Russian Federation	17,110
Italy	15,466	People's Republic of China	7,498
The Netherlands	7,479	Ukraine	2,923
Russian Federation	6,747	Germany	2,270
France	5,633	United States	2,120
Switzerland	4,965	Italy	959
Austria	4,956	Republic of Korea	957
Turkey	3,229	Japan	905
Canada	3,080	Uzbekistan	817
Romania	3,034	Turkey	786
Ukraine	2,549	Belarus	676
Germany	1,838	France	584
United Kingdom	1,695	United Kingdom	579
Poland	1,632	Poland	470
Israel	1,536	India	336
Uzbekistan	1,344	Kyrgyz Republic	333
Japan	1,146	Brazil	298
Portugal	1,020	The Netherlands	280
Spain	768	Austria	268

Sources: Authors' calculations based on UN Comtrade statistics.

Figure A2.1 Kazakhstan: Major Exports and Imports

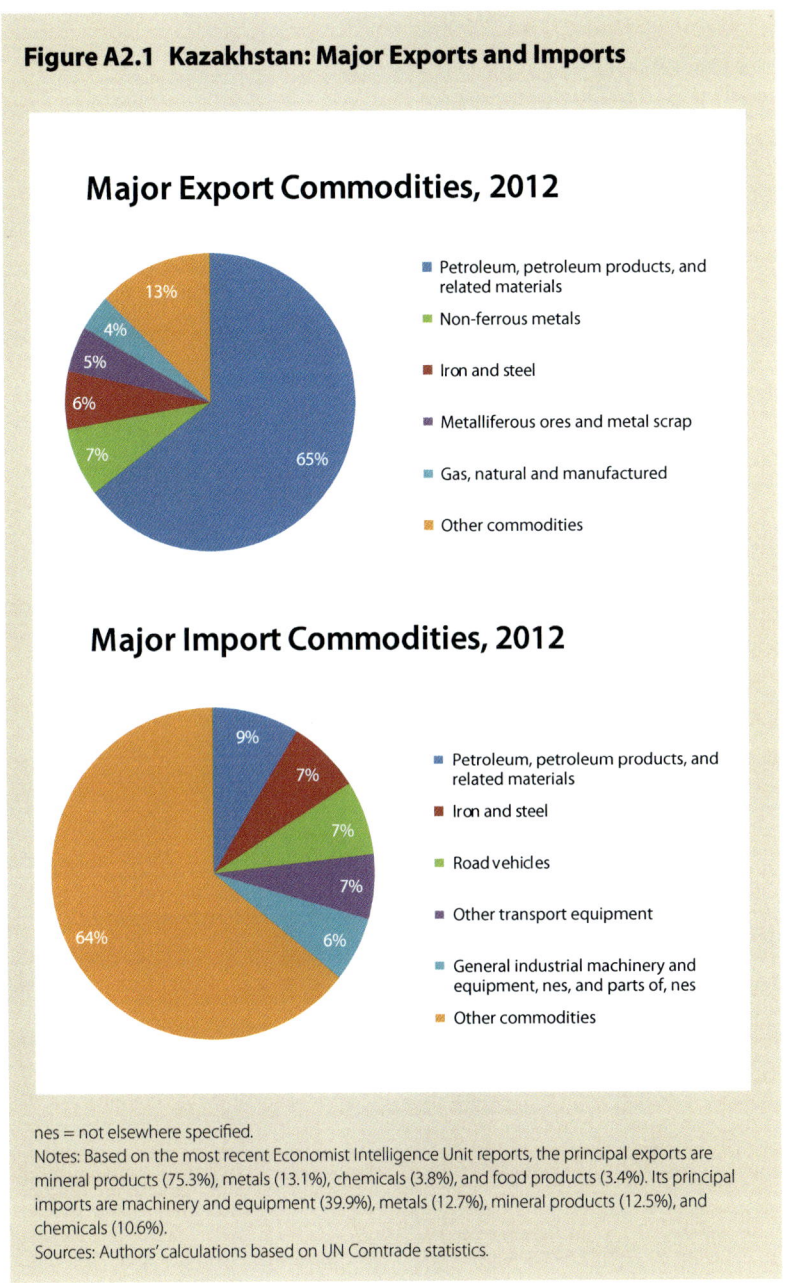

Major Export Commodities, 2012

- Petroleum, petroleum products, and related materials
- Non-ferrous metals
- Iron and steel
- Metalliferous ores and metal scrap
- Gas, natural and manufactured
- Other commodities

Major Import Commodities, 2012

- Petroleum, petroleum products, and related materials
- Iron and steel
- Road vehicles
- Other transport equipment
- General industrial machinery and equipment, nes, and parts of, nes
- Other commodities

nes = not elsewhere specified.
Notes: Based on the most recent Economist Intelligence Unit reports, the principal exports are mineral products (75.3%), metals (13.1%), chemicals (3.8%), and food products (3.4%). Its principal imports are machinery and equipment (39.9%), metals (12.7%), mineral products (12.5%), and chemicals (10.6%).
Sources: Authors' calculations based on UN Comtrade statistics.

Table A2.2 Kyrgyz Republic: Trading Partners, 2012
(exported and imported goods valued at US$10 million or more)

Trading Partner	Exports (US$ million)	Trading Partner	Imports (US$ million)
Switzerland	548	Russian Federation	1,785
Kazakhstan	405	People's Republic of China	1,210
Russian Federation	219	Kazakhstan	519
Uzbekistan	190	United States	253
People's Republic of China	61	Japan	216
Turkey	50	Germany	199
Tajikistan	40	Turkey	179
Afghanistan	26	Belarus	161
Germany	16	Ukraine	140
United Arab Emirates	16	Republic of Korea	92
British Virgin Islands	13	Uzbekistan	63
Belgium	13	The Netherlands	60
Belarus	11	Poland	36
		France	34
		United Kingdom	32
		India	30
		Sweden	28
		Canada	28
		Italy	20

Note: Based on the most recent Economist Intelligence Unit statistics, the main destinations of exports are Uzbekistan (12.7%), the Russian Federation (9.7%), Kazakhstan (11.1%), and the People's Republic of China (3.9%). The main origins of imports are the Russian Federation (29.3%), the People's Republic of China (19.5%), Kazakhstan (13.1%), and Belarus (4.7%).

Sources: Authors' calculations based on UN Comtrade statistics.

Figure A2.2 Kyrgyz Republic: Major Exports and Imports

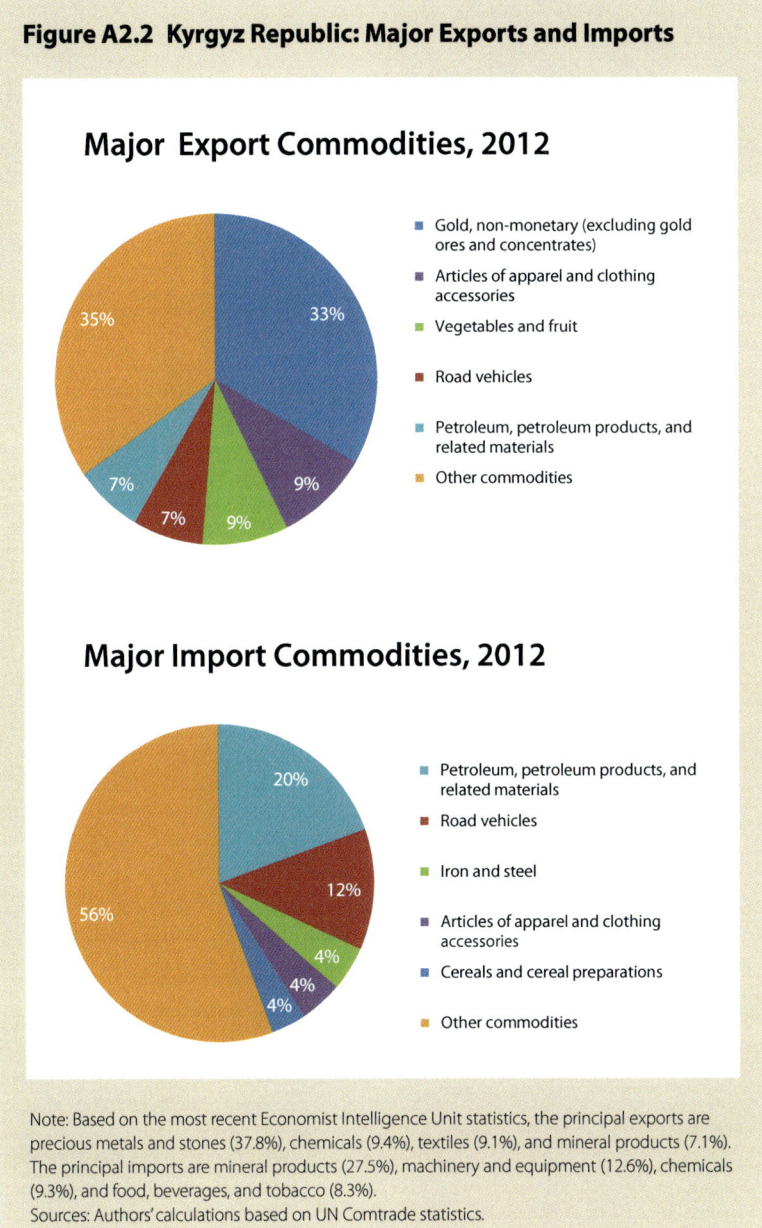

Major Export Commodities, 2012

- 33%
- 35%
- 7%
- 7%
- 9%
- 9%

Legend:
- Gold, non-monetary (excluding gold ores and concentrates)
- Articles of apparel and clothing accessories
- Vegetables and fruit
- Road vehicles
- Petroleum, petroleum products, and related materials
- Other commodities

Major Import Commodities, 2012

- 20%
- 12%
- 4%
- 4%
- 4%
- 56%

Legend:
- Petroleum, petroleum products, and related materials
- Road vehicles
- Iron and steel
- Articles of apparel and clothing accessories
- Cereals and cereal preparations
- Other commodities

Note: Based on the most recent Economist Intelligence Unit statistics, the principal exports are precious metals and stones (37.8%), chemicals (9.4%), textiles (9.1%), and mineral products (7.1%). The principal imports are mineral products (27.5%), machinery and equipment (12.6%), chemicals (9.3%), and food, beverages, and tobacco (8.3%).
Sources: Authors' calculations based on UN Comtrade statistics.

Table A2.3 Tajikistan: Trading Partners, 2012
(exported and imported goods valued at US$10 million or more)

Trading Partner	Exports (US$ million)	Trading Partner	Imports (US$ million)
Turkey	314	People's Republic of China	1,923
People's Republic of China	99	Russian Federation	738
Iran	77	Kazakhstan	416
Afghanistan	61	Turkey	258
Bangladesh	54	Iran	197
Kazakhstan	46	Turkmenistan	98
Russian Federation	45	United Arab Emirates	85
Italy	33	Uzbekistan	84
Norway	31	Ukraine	69
United States	25	Lithuania	67
Greece	22	United States	59
Pakistan	18	Belarus	53
The Netherlands	18	Afghanistan	47
India	15	Republic of Korea	42
Ukraine	12	Germany	38
Uzbekistan	10	Azerbaijan	36
		India	32
		Poland	23
		Venezuela	18
		Italy	18
		Kyrgyz Republic	18
		Latvia	12
		Austria	12

Note: Based on the latest Economist Intelligence Unit statistics, the main destinations of exports are the People's Republic of China (37.4%), Turkey (31.5%), Iran (5.0%), Afghanistan (4.4%), and Kazakhstan (1.7%). The main origins of imports are the Russian Federation (32.2%), Kazakhstan (11%), the People's Republic of China (9.0%), Iran (5.3%), and Turkey (2.3%).

Sources: Authors' calculations based on International Monetary Fund Direction of Trade Statistics.

Figure A2.3 Tajikistan: Major Exports and Imports

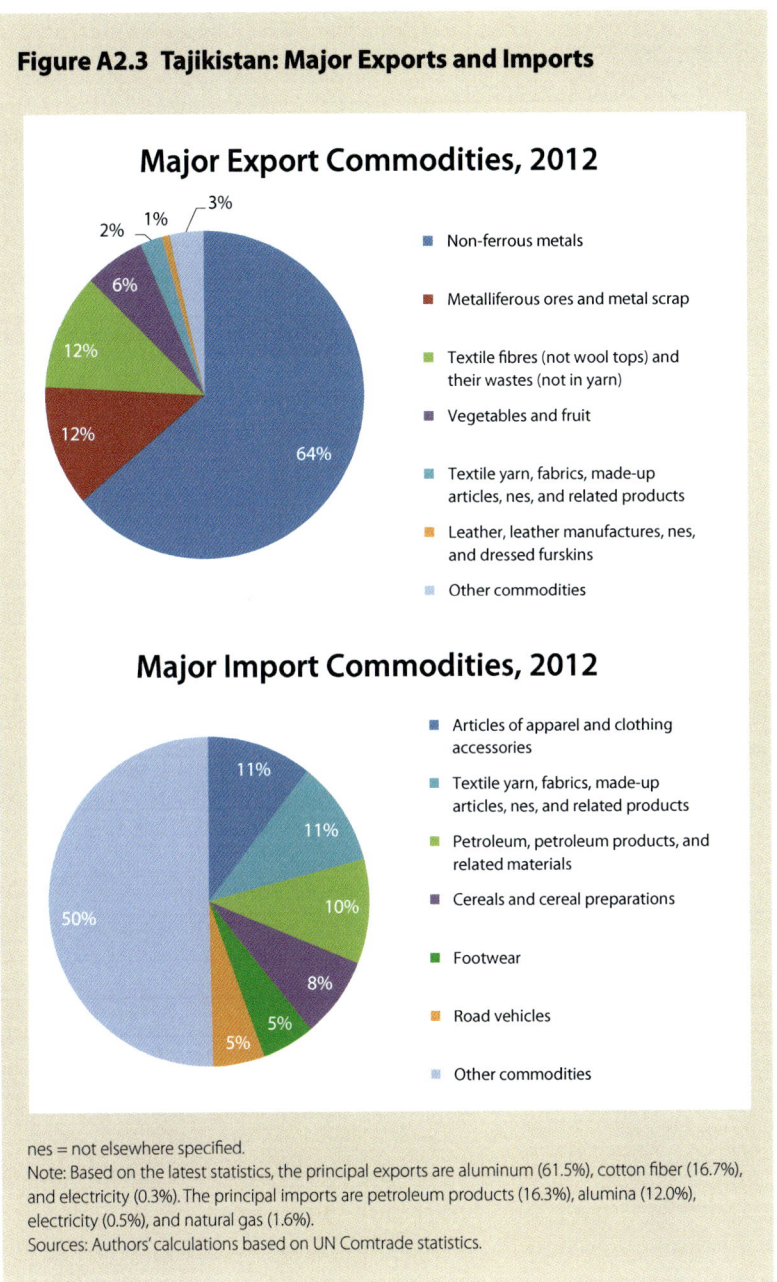

Major Export Commodities, 2012

- Non-ferrous metals
- Metalliferous ores and metal scrap
- Textile fibres (not wool tops) and their wastes (not in yarn)
- Vegetables and fruit
- Textile yarn, fabrics, made-up articles, nes, and related products
- Leather, leather manufactures, nes, and dressed furskins
- Other commodities

Major Import Commodities, 2012

- Articles of apparel and clothing accessories
- Textile yarn, fabrics, made-up articles, nes, and related products
- Petroleum, petroleum products, and related materials
- Cereals and cereal preparations
- Footwear
- Road vehicles
- Other commodities

nes = not elsewhere specified.
Note: Based on the latest statistics, the principal exports are aluminum (61.5%), cotton fiber (16.7%), and electricity (0.3%). The principal imports are petroleum products (16.3%), alumina (12.0%), electricity (0.5%), and natural gas (1.6%).
Sources: Authors' calculations based on UN Comtrade statistics.

Table A2.4 Turkmenistan: Trading Partners, 2012
(exported and imported goods valued at US$10 million or more)

Trading Partner	Exports (US$ million)	Trading Partner	Imports (US$ million)
People's Republic of China	7,290	People's Republic of China	1,870
Ukraine	698	Turkey	1,628
Italy	489	Russian Federation	1,209
United Arab Emirates	328	United Arab Emirates	658
Turkey	276	Germany	448
Afghanistan	251	United Kingdom	408
Iran	219	Iran	322
Russian Federation	165	Ukraine	277
Bangladesh	155	Belarus	255
Bermuda	144	Italy	228
United Kingdom	105	France	223
Germany	89	Republic of Korea	213
Tajikistan	89	Uzbekistan	157
United States	86	Kazakhstan	148
Kazakhstan	64	Japan	133
Georgia	53	The Netherlands	120
Uzbekistan	37	United States	94
Bulgaria	37	Gibraltar	94
Albania	34	India	77
Switzerland	27	Saudi Arabia	74
France	24	Azerbaijan	62
Armenia	13	Austria	60
Egypt	12	Canada	55

Note: Based on the latest Economist Intelligence Unit statistics, the main destinations of exports are the People's Republic of China (9.2%), the United Arab Emirates (2.3%), Italy (1.7%), and Ukraine (0.3%). The main origins of imports are Turkey (15.4%), the Russian Federation (9.7%), the People's Republic of China (7.1%), and the United Arab Emirates (5.9%). Exports to Iran and the Russian Federation are likely to be underestimates.

Sources: Authors' calculations based on International Monetary Fund Direction of Trade Statistics.

Figure A2.4 Turkmenistan: Major Exports and Imports

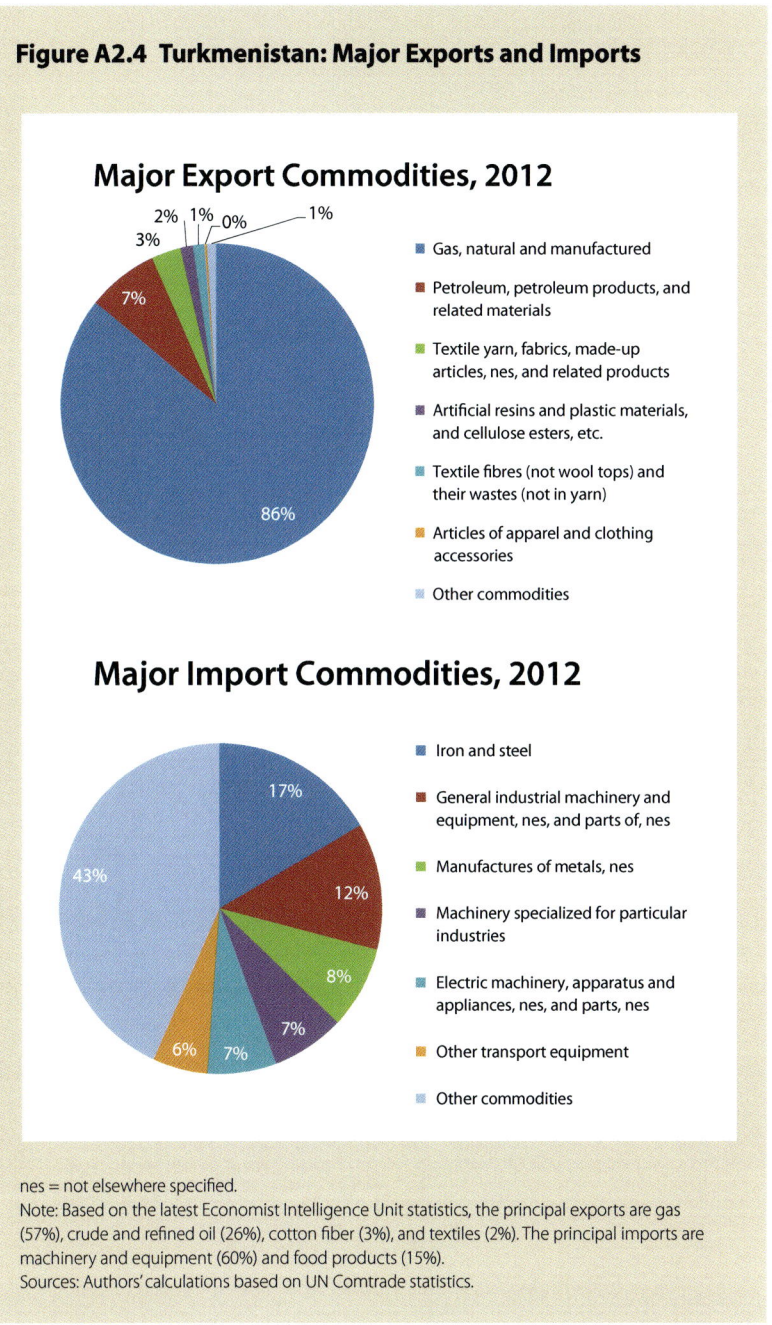

Major Export Commodities, 2012

- Gas, natural and manufactured
- Petroleum, petroleum products, and related materials
- Textile yarn, fabrics, made-up articles, nes, and related products
- Artificial resins and plastic materials, and cellulose esters, etc.
- Textile fibres (not wool tops) and their wastes (not in yarn)
- Articles of apparel and clothing accessories
- Other commodities

Major Import Commodities, 2012

- Iron and steel
- General industrial machinery and equipment, nes, and parts of, nes
- Manufactures of metals, nes
- Machinery specialized for particular industries
- Electric machinery, apparatus and appliances, nes, and parts, nes
- Other transport equipment
- Other commodities

nes = not elsewhere specified.
Note: Based on the latest Economist Intelligence Unit statistics, the principal exports are gas (57%), crude and refined oil (26%), cotton fiber (3%), and textiles (2%). The principal imports are machinery and equipment (60%) and food products (15%).
Sources: Authors' calculations based on UN Comtrade statistics.

Table A2.5 Uzbekistan: Trading Partners, 2012
(exported and imported goods valued at US$10 million or more)

Trading Partner	Exports (US$ million)	Trading Partner	Imports (US$ million)
People's Republic of China	992	Russian Federation	2,457
Turkey	739	People's Republic of China	1,962
Kazakhstan	713	Republic of Korea	1,943
Russian Federation	689	Kazakhstan	1,379
Ukraine	610	Germany	544
Bangladesh	445	Turkey	495
Kyrgyz Republic	189	Ukraine	406
Turkmenistan	142	Kyrgyz Republic	331
Iran	122	United States	313
Japan	96	Italy	154
Tajikistan	76	Poland	124
United Kingdom	39	Austria	123
Republic of Korea	39	India	121
India	31	Japan	108
Poland	28	Belarus	104
Belarus	26	France	94
United States	24	Czech Republic	87
Germany	14	Switzerland	77
Italy	12	The Netherlands	74
Azerbaijan	12	Hungary	73
France	11	United Kingdom	65
Georgia	11	Malaysia	64
Egypt	11	Lithuania	52

Note: Based on the latest Economist Intelligence Unit statistics, the main destinations of exports are the People's Republic of China (18.5%), Kazakhstan (14.6%), Turkey (13.8%), the Russian Federation (12.8%), Ukraine (12.5%), and Bangladesh (8.9%). The main origins of imports are the Russian Federation (20.6%), the People's Republic of China (16.5%), the Republic of Korea (16.3%), Kazakhstan (12.8%), Germany (4.6%), and Turkey (4.2%).
Sources: Authors' calculations based on International Monetary Fund Direction of Trade Statistics.

Figure A2.5 Uzbekistan: Major Exports and Imports

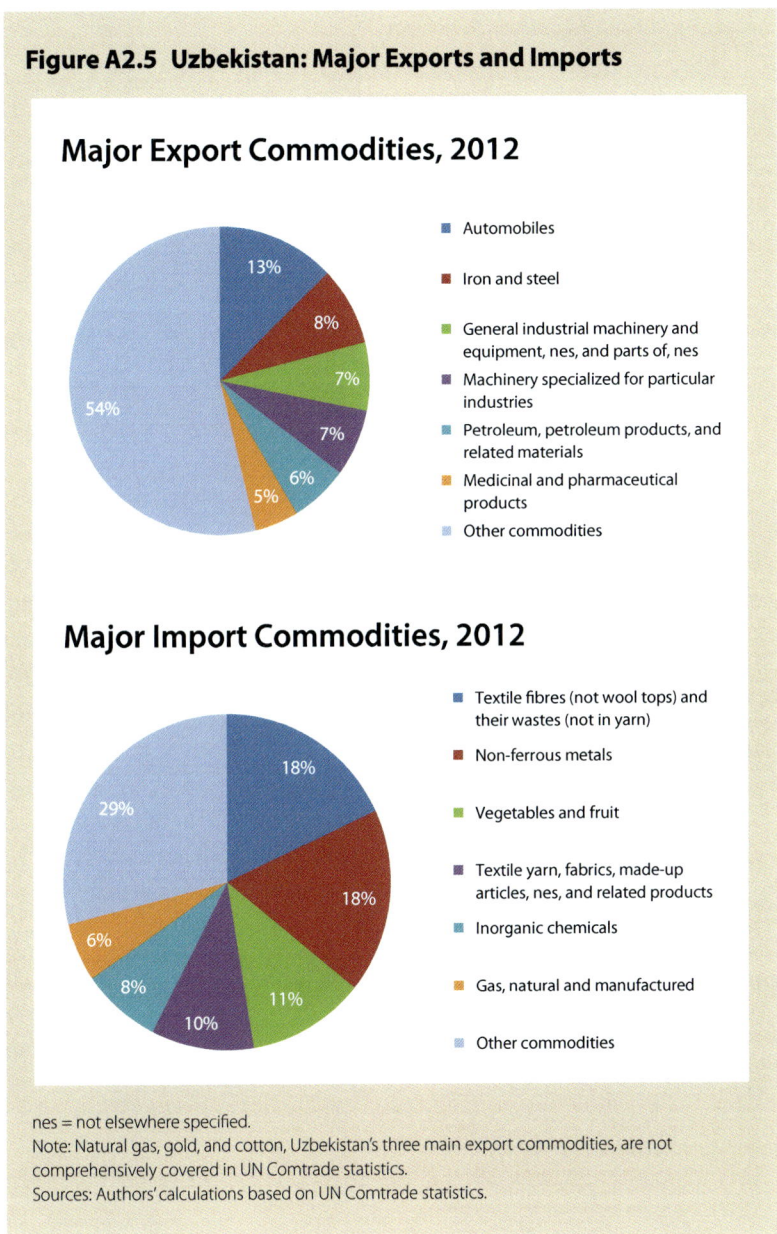

Major Export Commodities, 2012

- Automobiles
- Iron and steel
- General industrial machinery and equipment, nes, and parts of, nes
- Machinery specialized for particular industries
- Petroleum, petroleum products, and related materials
- Medicinal and pharmaceutical products
- Other commodities

Major Import Commodities, 2012

- Textile fibres (not wool tops) and their wastes (not in yarn)
- Non-ferrous metals
- Vegetables and fruit
- Textile yarn, fabrics, made-up articles, nes, and related products
- Inorganic chemicals
- Gas, natural and manufactured
- Other commodities

nes = not elsewhere specified.
Note: Natural gas, gold, and cotton, Uzbekistan's three main export commodities, are not comprehensively covered in UN Comtrade statistics.
Sources: Authors' calculations based on UN Comtrade statistics.

Appendix 3
Quantitative Assessment: Trade Gravity Model

Table A3.1 reports regression estimates on the relationship between trade (exports, imports, and total trade), distance, economic size, and standard controls for institutional and cultural ties (included, but not reported), using year 2011 data 4-digit SITC Rev. 2 (Tables A1.1 and A1.2 provide data sources and industry list). The standard controls are the gross domestic product of the country pairs; a dummy for pairs of countries that share a common border, speak the same language, and share a common colonial link. The estimation follows Helpman, Melitz, and Rubinstein (2008). A similar estimation for Eurasian trade can be found in Gill et al. (2014, 95), although without factor endowment, infrastructure, and trade facilitation controls. The variables are estimated in logs (except for dummy variables). The regression method is ordinary least squares. Standard errors are in parentheses, with *** (**, *) denoting statistical significance at 1% (5%, 10%).

Table A3.1 Trade Gravity Estimation for Central Asia

Dependent Variable ≡ log (Bilateral Trade)	Coefficient (standard error)	Dependent Variable ≡ log (Bilateral Trade)	Coefficient (standard error)
Log (distance)	−0.21	Regulation Costs	1.52
	(0.131)		(7.037)
Log (Home GDP)	−5.903	Home Infrastructure Quality	9.843
	(0.359)***		(0.812)***
Log (Destination GDP)	−0.656	Trade Facilitation Performance	−0.031
	(0.321)**		−0.073
Log|Difference in Per Capita GDP|	−2.527	Dummy for ASEAN excl. CLMV Trading Partners	−4.162
	(0.183)***		(0.704)***
Common border dummy	−3.605	Dummy for ASEAN CLMV Trading Partners	0
	(0.318)***		(.)
Common language dummy	−0.195	Dummy for South Asia Trading Partners	−6.099
	(0.142)		(0.290)***
Common colonizer dummy	−2.835	Dummy for Central Asia Trading Partners	2.326
	(0.231)***		(0.235)***
Log|Difference In Capital/Labor|	38.045	R–sq.	0.71
	(2.392)***	Observations	3,056

ASEAN = Association of Southeast Asian Nations; CLMV = Cambodia, Lao People's Democratic Republic, Myanmar, and Viet Nam; GDP = gross domestic product.

115

References

Abdih, Y., and L. Medina. 2013. Measuring the Informal Economy in the Caucasus and Central Asia. IMF Working Paper No. 13/137.

Agency on Statistics under President of the Republic of Tajikistan. http://www.stat.tj/en/ (accessed 3 January 2014).

Agency of Statistics of the Republic of Kazakhstan. http://www.stat.gov.kz/ (accessed 3 January 2014).

Asian Development Bank (ADB). 2006. *Central Asia: Increasing Gains from Trade through Regional Cooperation in Trade Policy, Transport and Customs Transit.* Manila: ADB.

Asian Development Bank. 2013a. *Asian Development Outlook (ADO): Asia's Energy Challenge.* Manila: ADB.

Asian Development Bank. 2013b. *CAREC Corridor Performance Monitoring and Measurement. Annual Report 2012.* Manila: ADB.

Asian Development Bank. 2013c. *Key Indicators for Asia and the Pacific 2013.* Manila: ADB.

Asian Development Bank. 2014. *Asian Development Outlook (ADO): Economic Trends and Prospects in Developing Asia - Central Asia.* Manila: ADB.

Barabasi, A.-L., R. Hausmann, C. A. Hidalgo, and B. Klinger. 2007. The Product Space Conditions the Development of Nations. *Science* 27(5837): 482–487.

Beck, S., S. Shinozaki, Q. Zhang, and E. Mangampat. 2013. Asian Development Bank Trade Finance Survey: Major Findings. ADB Briefs No. 11. Manila: ADB.

Berlemann, M., and J-E. Wesselhoft. 2012. Estimating Aggregate Capital Stocks Using the Perpetual Inventory Method – New Empirical Evidence for 103 Countries. Helmut Schmidt University Hamburg. Working Paper No. 125.

Bernard, A.B., S.J. Redding, and P.K. Schott. 2007. Comparative Advantage and Heterogeneous Firms. *Review of Economic Studies* 74: 31–66.

Birkman, L., M. Kaloshnika, M. Khan, U. Shavurov, and S. Smallhouse. 2012. *Textile and Apparel Cluster in Kyrgyz Republic.* Cambridge, MA: Harvard University Kennedy School and Harvard Business School. http://www.isc.hbs. edu/pdf/Student_Projects/2012%20MOC%20Papers/Kyrgyz Republic_Textile%20and%20Apparel%20Cluster_Final_May%204%202012.pdf (accessed 5 May 2014).

Böcking, D. 2013. Deutsch-Chinesische Güterstrecke: Moin, Moin, Weltwirtschaftslok. *Der Spiegel*, 2 August.

Bradsher, K. 2013. Hauling New Treasures along the Silk Road. *The New York Times*, 20 July.

Cadot, O., C. Carrère, and C. Grigoriou 2006. *Landlockedness, Infrastructure and Trade in Central Asia.* Washington, DC: World Bank.

Central Asia Regional Economic Cooperation (CAREC). 2012. *Corridor Performance Measurement and Monitoring Annual Report 2012.* http://cfcfa.net/cpmm/cpmm-annual- and-quarterly-reports/2012-annual-report/ (accessed 15 November 2013).

Cohen, E. 1979. Rethinking the Sociology of Tourism. *Annals of Tourism Research* 6(1): 18–35.

Danzer, A., and O. Ivaschenko. 2010. Migration Patterns in a Remittances Dependent Economy: Evidence from Tajikistan during the Global Financial Crisis. *Migration Letters* 7(2): 190–202.

Djamankulov, N. 2011. SPS Regulations and Access of Kyrgyz Goods to the Customs Union. USAID Regional Trade Liberalization and Customs Project (USAID Contract No. 176-C-00-07-00011-08), Bishkek.

Doing Business. http://www.doingbusiness.org/ (accessed 3 January 2014).

Dowling, M., and G. Wignaraja. 2006a. Central Asia's Economy: Mapping Future Prospects to 2015. Silk Road Paper Series. Central Asia-Caucasus Institute, Silk Road Studies Program, Johns Hopkins University-SAIS.

Dowling, M., and G. Wignaraja. 2006b. Central Asia after Fifteen Years of Transition: Growth, Regional Cooperation, and Policy Choices. *Asia-Pacific Development Journal* 13(2): 113–144.

Dunning, J. 1993. *Multinational Enterprises and the Global Economy. Reading*, MA: Addison-Wesley.

Egert, B. 2013. Dutch Disease in the Post-Soviet Countries of Central and South-West Asia: How Contagious Is It? CESIFO Working Paper No. 4186.

Eurasian Development Bank. 2013. Monitoring of Direct Investments of Belarus, Kazakhstan, Russia and Ukraine in Eurasia. Centre for Integration Studies, Report No. 19.

European Bank for Reconstruction and Development (EBRD). 2012. *Regional Trade Integration and the Eurasian Economic Union, Transition Report 2012.* London: EBRD.

fDi Intelligence. 2013. *The fDi Report 2013: Global Greenfield Investment Trends.* The Financial Times Ltd.

Fujita, M., P. Krugman, and A.J. Venables. 1999. *The Spatial Economy: Cities, Regions, and International Trade.* London, UK: MIT Press.

Gill, I.S., I. Izvorski, W. van Eeghen, and D. De Rosa. 2014. *Diversified Development: Making the Most of Natural Resources in Eurasia.* Washington, DC: World Bank.

Government of the Kyrgyz Republic. 2013a. Export Development Strategy of Kyrgyz Republic. Draft (in Russian). http://www.mineconom.kg/images/files/trade/strategia.docx (accessed 14 June 2014).

Government of the Kyrgyz Republic. 2013b. Programme of Development of Textile and Sewing Production of the Kyrgyz Republic for 2013-2015.

Grafe, C., M. Raiser, and T. Sakatsume. 2008. Beyond Borders – Reconsidering Regional Trade in Central Asia. *Journal of Comparative Economics* 36(3): 453–466.

Grigoriou, C. 2007. Landlockedness, Infrastructure and Trade: New Estimates for Central Asian Countries. Policy Research Working Paper 4335. Washington, DC: World Bank.

Gunn, C. 1988. *Tourism Planning*, 2nd ed. New York: Taylor and Francis.

Hamilton, J.D. 2013. Oil Prices, Exhaustible Resources, and Economic Growth. In *Handbook of Energy and Climate Change*, edited by R. Fouquet. Glocs, UK: Edward Elgar.

Hanson, G.H., and C. Xiang. 2004. The Home-Market Effect and Bilateral Trade Patterns. *American Economic Review* 94: 1108–1129.

Helpman, E. 2011. *Understanding Global Trade*. Cambridge, MA: Harvard University Press.

Helpman, E., M. Melitz, and Y. Rubinstein. 2008. Estimating Trade Flows: Trading Partners and Trading Volumes. *Quarterly Journal of Economics* 123(2): 441–487.

Idrisov, G., and B. Taganov. 2013. Regional Trade Integration in the CIS Area. Munich Personal RePec Archive Paper No.50952. http://mpra.ub.uni-muenchen.de/50952/ (accessed 5 May 2014)

International Air Transport Association (IATA). 2014. Air Freight Market Analysis, February 2014. http://www.iata.org/whatwedo/Documents/economics/freight-analysis-feb-2014.pdf (accessed 14 June 2014).

International Labour Organization (ILO). 2010a. Migrant Remittances to Tajikistan. The Potential for Savings, Economic Investment and Existing Financial Products to Attract Remittances. Moscow: ILO.

International Labour Organization. 2010b. *Migration and Development in Tajikistan: Emigration, Return and Diaspora*. Moscow: ILO.

International Labour Organization. 2012. Skills for Trade and Economic Diversification in the Kyrgyz Garment Sector. Employment Report No. 19.

Inskeep, E. 1991. *Tourism Planning: An Integrated and Sustainable Development Approach*. New York: Van Nostrand Reinhold.

Kemme, D. 2012. Sovereign Wealth Fund Issues and the National Fund(s) of Kazakhstan. Working Paper 1036. Ann Arbor, MI: William Davidson Institute, University of Michigan.

Kosimova, L. 2014. Charo Todzhikon Rub A Mokhodzhirati Mekhnati Ovardaand? Muhochir Magazine, No. 04(44), 27 March. Migration Service of the Ministry of Labor, Migration and Employment of the Population of the Republic of Tajikistan.

Krugman, P. 1998. What Happened to Asia? Unpublished paper. http://web.mit.edu/krugman/www/DISINTER.html. (accessed 5 May 2014).

Kulipanova, E. 2012. International Transport in Central Asia: Understanding the Patterns of (Non-) Cooperation. University of Central Asia Institute of Public Policy and Administration. Working Paper No. 2.

Laruelle, M., and S. Peyrouse. 2012. Regional Organisations in Central Asia: Patterns of Interaction, Dilemmas of Efficiency. University of Central Asia Institute of Public Policy and Administration. Working Paper No. 10.

Leamer, E.E. 1987. Paths of Development in the Three-Factor, n-Good General Equilibrium Model. *Journal of Political Economy* 95(5): 961-999.

Leamer, E.E., and R.M. Stern. 2009. *Quantitative International Economics*. London, UK: Transaction Publishers.

Lee, H.Y., L.A. Ricci, and R. Rigobon. 2004. Once Again, Is Openness Good for Growth? *Journal of Development Economics* 75(2): 451–472.

Libman, A., and E. Vinokurov. 2012. *Holding-Together Regionalism: Twenty Years of Post-Soviet Integration*. Basingstoke, UK: Palgrave Macmillan.

Linn, J. 2004. *Economic (Dis)Integration Matters: The Soviet Collapse Revisited*. Washington, DC: Brookings Institution.

Marat, E. 2009. Labor Migration in Central Asia: Implications of the Global Economic Crisis. Silk Road Paper Series. Central Asia-Caucasus Institute, Silk Road Studies Program, Johns Hopkins University-SAIS.

Mogilevskii, R. 2012a. Customs Union of Belarus, Kazakhstan and Russia: Trade Creation and Trade Diversion in Central Asia in 2010–2011. University of Central Asia Institute of Public Policy and Administration. Working Paper No. 12.

Mogilevskii, R. 2012b. Re-export Activities in Kyrgyz Republic: Issues and Prospects. University of Central Asia Institute of Public Policy and Administration. Working Paper No. 9.

Mogilevskii, R. 2012c. Trends and Patterns in Foreign Trade of Central Asian Countries. University of Central Asia Institute of Public Policy and Administration. Working Paper No. 1.

National Bank of Kazakhstan. http://www.nationalbank.kz/?switch=eng (accessed 3 January 2014).

National Bank of the Kyrgyz Republic. http://www.nbkr.kg/ (accessed 3 January 2014).

National Statistical Committee of the Kyrgyz Republic. http://www.stat.kg/ (accessed 3 January 2014).

Olimova, S. 2010. The Impact of Labour Migration on Human Capital: The Case of Tajikistan. *Revue Européenne des Migrations Internationales* 26(3): 181–197.

Olimova, S. 2014. http://rus.ozodi.org/content/article/25329522.html (accessed 28 April 2014).

Organisation for Economic Co-operation and Development (OECD). 2014. Expanding the Garment Industry in the Kyrgyz Republic. Policy Handbook. http://www.oecd.org/globalrelations/psd/ExpandingtheGarmentIndustry.pdf (accessed 14 June 2014).

Pomfret, R. 2001. *The Economics of Regional Trading Arrangements*. Oxford, UK: Oxford University Press.

Pomfret, R. 2009. Regional Integration in Central Asia. *Economic Change and Restructuring* 42(1–2): 47–68.

Raballand, G. 2003. Determinants of the Negative Impact of Being Landlocked on Trade: An Empirical Investigation through the Central Asian Case. *Comparative Economic Studies* 45(4): 520–36.

Rauch, J.E. 1999. Networks versus Markets in International Trade. *Journal of International Economics* 48(1): 7–35.

Romalis, J. 2004. Factor Proportions and the Structure of Commodity Trade. *American Economic Review* 94: 67–97.

Sabyrova, L. 2009. A Wedge Between Two Output Measures: What Does It Tell Us? RAKURS Center for Economic Analysis. Macroeconomic Notes, No. 1.2.

Schwabe, G., J. Novak, and M. Aggeler. 2008. Designing the Tourist Agency of the Future. Paper presented at the 21st Bled eConference, Bled, Slovenia, 15-18 June. https://domino.fov.uni-mb.si/proceedings.nsf/0/905026288c017bd0c1257481003c7ce8/$file/04schwabe.pdf (retrieved June 2014).

Seetanah, B., T.D. Juwaheer, M.J. Lamport, S. Rojid, R.V. Sannassee, and U. Subadar Agathee. 2011. Does Infrastructure Matter in Tourism Development? *University of Mauritius Research Journal* 17(1): 89-108.

Shepotylo, O., and D. Tarr. 2012. Impact of WTO Accession and the Customs Union on the Bound and Applied Tariff Rates of the Russian Federation. Policy Research Working Paper 6161. Washington, DC: World Bank.

SIAR Research & Consulting. 2011. *Status and Prospects of the Kyrgyz Garment Sewing Industry.* Bishkek: USAID.

Smeral, E. 1993. Aspects to Justify Public Tourism Promotion: An Economic Perspective. *Tourism Review* 61(3): 6-14.

State Committee of the Republic of Uzbekistan on Statistics. http://www.stat.uz/en/index.php (accessed 3 January 2014).

Summers, T. 2013. Still "Going West"? *East Asia Forum Quarterly* 5(3): 25-26.

Umarov, K. 2010. Tajik Labor Migration during the Global Economic Crisis: Causes and Consequences. Research report. Dushanbe: ILO.

United Nations Conference on Trade and Development (UNCTAD). 2013. *World Investment Report 2013: Global Value Chains: Investment and Trade for Development.* Geneva: United Nations.

UNCTADstat. http://unctadstat.unctad.org/ReportFolders/reportFolders.aspx?sCS_referer=&sCS_ChosenLang=en (accessed 3 January 2014).

United Nations Development Programme (UNDP). 2005. *Central Asia Human Development Report: Bringing Down Barriers: Regional Cooperation for Human Development and Human Security.* Bratislava, Slovakia: UNDP.

United Nations World Tourism Organization (UNWTO). 2014. International Tourism Generates US$1.4 Trillion in Export Earnings. *UNWTO World Tourism Barometer.* Volume 12, April.

United States Agency for International Development (USAID) Local Development Program. 2011. Assessment of the Textile Sector in Kyrgyz Republic. http://ldp.kg/wp-content/uploads/2012/07/Textile-Sector-Assessment-2011.pdf (accessed 14 June 2014).

World Bank. World Development Indicators. http://databank.worldbank.org/data/home.aspx (accessed 3 January 2014).

World Economic Forum. 2013. *Global Competitiveness Report 2013–2014*, Full Data Edition. Geneva: World Economic Forum.

World Trade Organization. 2013. Trade Policy Review: Kyrgyz Republic. Report by the Secretariat, WT/TPR/S/288, 1 October. http://www.wto.org/english/tratop_e/tpr_e/s288_e.pdf (accessed 5 May 2014).

Z/Yen Group. 2014. The Global Financial Centres Index 15. http://www.longfinance.net/images/GFCI15_15March2014.pdf (accessed 14 June 2014).